Live By Design
Not by Default

Being an effective Christian

Jim Dunn

malcolm down
PUBLISHING

ENDORSEMENTS

Jim Dunn has been a passionate, and respected affiliate of The Pacific Institute for many years. His commitment to help people be their best has been truly inspiring and very impactful. With his new book, Jim provides a valuable resource as he continues in that quest.
Scott Sproull, CEO
The Pacific Institute, LLC

Over the last 20 years a stronger Kingdom approach has encouraged Christians not just to develop spiritually and personally but to believe that Christians really can become major players in God's purposes within his world. This book by Jim Dunn is addressing this shift of thinking and from his experience within the business and industrial world encourages the reader towards higher ground.
Stuart Bell
Senior Pastor of Alive Church and leader of the Ground Level Net

Jim has been involved in a wide range of leadership – both Christian and secular – for a large part of his life. In this book he shares the experience of many years. He distils that experience into a number of straightforward but profound challenges, starting with the question, 'If you could change just one thing about your life right now, what would it be?' I commend this book to anyone seeking to grow in their personal and spiritual life.
Neil Wardrope
CLC International

The title of this book Live By Design, Not By Default *offers to every believer a balanced, thoroughly practical and biblical nudge towards a victorious lifestyle, a life which pleases Him and one which is more likely to deal with the inevitable conflict that arises in the experience of the believer. It does not, however, join the ranks of numerous 'self-help manuals' which abound wherever you look. Rather it is an invitation to a somewhat different avenue to life and liberty in Christ.*

Jim Dunn enjoys many gifts of the Holy Spirit and one that stands out is in the field of communication whether in preaching, teaching, lecturing to kings and presidents, writing or simply communicating a great truth to one person. In this book Jim Dunn has succeeded in taking the truths inherent in sound theology and the behavioural sciences, discerning and merging them into a meaningful whole in a unique way. In this the text stands alone and available to every person desiring to deepen the relationship with their Lord and Saviour. It may also lead some to faith for the first time or restore a dying ember into life and fire.

I commend this work without hesitation and pray God's blessing upon it as it becomes an instrument of divinely inspired change.

Dr John Birch, OBE, PhD, MEd

Author of *Conflict in the Church, A Pastoral Perspective*

First published in 2019 by Malcolm Down Publishing Ltd
www.malcolmdown.co.uk

British Library Cataloguing in Publication Data
A catalogue record for this book is available from the British Library.
ISBN: 978-1-910786-40-6

Cover design by Esther Kotecha

Art direction by Sarah Grace

Printed in the UK

'Live life, then, with a due sense of responsibility, not as men who do not know the meaning and purpose of life but as those who do. Make the best use of your time despite all the difficulties of these days. Don't be vague, but firmly grasp what you know to be the will of God.'

(Paul: letter to the Ephesians 5:15–16, PHILLIPS)

Contents

Jim Dunn is a long-term church leader and business professional who currently serves on his local church leadership team.

His vision is to preach and teach the Word of God in ways that focus on its life-changing power. He conducts Life Change workshops and key issue seminars and brings regular Bible teaching on important, life-related topics and is widely recognised as a communicator and skills developer.

His background is in Engineering and Behavioural Psychology. He is an associate of the Royal College of Science and Technology and a graduate of Glasgow University.

Following a lengthy career in the UK steel industry he now consults with businesses, educational establishments, local communities and churches in the UK and in Europe working with individuals and groups to bring positive change through the application of Christian principles.

He serves on the International Board of the 'Way of Hope Foundation', a Christian voluntary organisation based in Budapest, and is dedicated to working with orphans and other disadvantaged youngsters throughout Hungary, Ukraine, Serbia and Croatia.

He is the author of several books including *The Effective Leader*, *The Life Wise Guide to Work*, *God's Wisdom for Your Money* and a fiction series for teenagers.

FOREWORD

As a church pastor for over forty years the thing that has perhaps caused me the greatest pain has been to do with Christians living at a lower level of life than God intended. People who began their journey with a sense of vibrancy and life who later made poor choices leading to disastrous results. For some this was unmet expectations and broken relationships; for others even loss of faith and a turning away from church life.

I believe that historically part of the problem lies with the church who failed to lift people into their full potential. A sacred-secular divide isolated believers into a world where, within the church, a kind of private religion could easily develop which limited people's effectiveness and confined them in small-church thinking.

Thankfully, over the last twenty years a stronger Kingdom approach has encouraged Christians not just to develop spiritually and personally but to believe that Christians really can become major players in God's purposes within his world.

This book by Jim Dunn is addressing this shift of thinking, and from his experience within the business and industrial world encourages the reader towards higher ground. This is both theologically grounded and practically accessible for all. It is not a self-help proposal, but it is filled with wise advice towards a greater and more adventurous trust in a God who offers life in all its fullness.

An intentional change of thinking will prove to be inspirational, challenging and effective, moving the reader beyond mediocrity and towards successful living.

Stuart Bell

Senior Pastor of Alive Church and leader of Ground Level Net

PREFACE

Some years ago a government-backed community transformation project was launched in Glasgow. It targeted an important if run down area of the city and was called 'The Govan Initiative'.[1]

The project addressed key social and economic issues and aimed to raise the aspirations of residents and bring significant improvements to the life and well-being of the community at every level and it met with measurable success.

I attended a conference at which delegates from The Govan Initiative presented the outcomes of their work. I vividly recall the words of one of their team, an ordinary, unremarkable woman with no particular talent for speaking. She was trying to get us to understand why this was such a good and important project. Referring to friends and neighbours and fellow residents from within her community she said, 'You see, they're all looking for something that will change their lives!'

Simple as that.

My work has taken me around the world and wherever I have gone I have found people from all walks of life expressing the same heartfelt desire. Whether it be the oil fields of north-west Canada, the political heartlands of southern Europe or here in the UK seems to make little difference.

I've worked with executives in the UK and Europe, with factory workers and educationalists, with serving police officers, prisoners in our young offender institutions, single parents struggling to bring up their families, and Christians in churches here in the UK and in Eastern Europe; one of the things I have repeatedly observed is the appetite people have for anything that they believe will make a positive difference to their lives.

I've been involved in church leadership for around forty years. During that time I've had the opportunity and privilege of observing and helping others as they've worked at their Christian lives in a variety of situations.

My vision has been, and still is, to preach and teach the Word of God in ways that focus upon its life-changing power because I believe that Christ Himself is the key to successful living and that what counts is not so much a strong belief in ourselves but a deep, active faith in Him.

Much of what I have seen and learned in my secular roles, and also while working and living among Christians, has revived a long-felt need for a practical book that could inspire us to rise to this challenge and show us how to become more *effective* in our lives and work.

Oliver Wendall Holmes Sr (1809–1894), the American poet, physician and essayist, made an insightful observation. He said, 'Many people die with their music still in them. Too often it is because they are always getting ready to live. Before they know it, time runs out'.[2]

If this is true for human beings in general then of how much greater significance must it be for the Christian? Being effective will mean different things to each of us and will most likely be defined by the circumstances in which we find ourselves and the way we deal with the challenges and opportunities that present themselves at the coal face of our lives. But setting practical outworkings aside for a moment, let it be said that in the final analysis, the key to our own personal effectiveness lies in cooperating with the Divine purpose and living the kind of life that is founded upon Christ's resources and power.

In every age and generation, truly effective people are the ones who have done this and the aim of this book is to show how you can do the same. The title *Live By Design, Not By Default* suggests this is not something that happens by accident or chance, but it is the result of deliberate, focused action of the right kind.

You don't need to have a personality transplant or possess a certain kind of charisma to be effective but there are certain things you must know and do consistently.

This book deals with these things. It is thoroughly biblical, theologically sound and immensely practical. It will take you on a journey that will lead to a deeper understanding of who you are and of what God is calling you to do and be.

It will challenge your current behaviour and make you aware of the spiritual and mental thought patterns and the habits that may be holding you back and which you need to change. Most of all, it will help you create your own agenda for change and enable you to move forward with your life in the truest and best sense of those words.

INTRODUCTION:
Time for Change

You have dwelt long enough at this mountain. (Deut. 1:6)

If you could change just one thing about your life right now, what would it be?

Most of us want to grow and develop, not just spiritually but across the whole spectrum of life. The desire to live fully is something that is deeply rooted within the heart of every human being. This lust for life is perhaps strongest when we are young. It's as if we sense the possibilities that lie before us and find ourselves instinctively reaching out, eager to lay hold of them for ourselves. During childhood we're in discovery mode, most of the time. We are inquisitive, energetic, eager to learn and do new things. We're not held back by suffocating self-doubt or fear. But as we enter adulthood something happens: it's called growing up.

The lines of a familiar old hymn say it with great poignancy:

And soon, too soon, the wintry hour
Of man's maturer age,
Will shake the soul with sorrow's power
And stormy passions rage![3]

We get caught up in the business of living; coping with its routines, solving its problems, earning a living, acquiring possessions. We readily acknowledge that there's more to life than simply

17

increasing its speed but at the same time we feel that there's not much we can do about it other than try to keep pace. It is strange that these influences should shape most of life for us and yet they do. They are not all bad; on the contrary, many of them are necessary and worthwhile. But the conditioning of daily life means that we slowly, unwittingly, change – not to succeed but to survive – in a way that gains the acceptance of others. We get by; we do what we must, as well as we can. We play our roles, do our jobs, put a little away for the future and, in some cases, simply hope for the best.

In the going, we tend to lose touch with the deep desires and aspirations of our earlier years. The dreams we dreamed as children we learn to no longer believe. At best we only sense them occasionally and the memory is distant and vague. If we remember them at all and reconnect with them, we may feel that they are somehow beyond us and simply dismiss them out of hand as things that are no longer possible for us.

Over time our aspirations shrink; our vision of what is possible for us becomes dimmer and more limited. Experience tends to blunt the edge of our idealism and we become more realistic. It's as if we learn to strike a bargain with life and settle for something less than we really wanted.

You may have come across the poem 'My Wage' by Jessie B. Rittenhouse. It is thought provoking and raises issues that deserve consideration.

I bargained with Life for a penny,
And Life would pay no more,
However I begged at evening
When I counted my scanty store:
For Life is a just employer,
He gives you what you ask,
But once you have set the wages,
Why, you must bear the task.
I worked for a menial's hire,
Only to learn, dismayed,
That any wage I had asked of Life,
Life would have paid.[4]

There's a trap that is easy to fall into; it happens when you limit your choices to what seems possible or reasonable for you. When you do this you tend to disconnect yourself from what you really want and then all that is left is a compromise.

One of the reasons why you are reading this book may be because there are still those times when you sense that much more is possible for you: you have not quite given up on that idea. But you may feel at a loss to know where to start or how to find the path that will lead you in the direction of what is right and good for you.

The market place is saturated with products claiming to help. The demand for books, CDs, DVDs, lectures and seminars dealing with these and other related topics is insatiable. But there is a downside to all of it since many of these offerings do not and cannot deliver what they promise and often leave the seeker disappointed and disillusioned.

One thing is certainly true: the things that chain you and me to history and shackle the forward movement of our lives can be dealt with, and we should at the very least encourage ourselves and others in the belief that we need not be stuck where we are or with who we are. But worldly wisdom and the adoption of worldly wise methods just don't provide the answers that are needed. For many years I have seen and felt the need for an organising principle in life, a principle that would enable us to get a handle on things, unravel confusion and get us to the bottom line, fast.

There is one perspective that puts everything else into its proper perspective. It is expressed through these thought-provoking words taken from the Old Testament book of Psalms: 'For with You is the fountain of life; in Your light we see light' (Ps. 36:9).

These are words that resonate, they 'roll off the tongue', but what exactly do they mean? Well, they refer to God Himself and to His way for us. They express a great principle of life and living and they surely cause us to think of Jesus Christ who said: 'I have come that they may have life, and that they may have it more abundantly' (John 10:10).

He is key, not only to life in the *hereafter* but also to life in the *here and now*. I reached that conclusion many years ago and nothing I have seen or heard or experienced in the interim has made me think I should change my mind. His words are as pertinent to all of us today as they were when He first uttered them. Following Him is a life-affirming, life-enhancing process that leads us towards being, doing and having all that God intends and only through Him can we live this kind of life.

The Space Where the 'Magic' Happens

In this book I am advocating a specific spiritual approach to life and its challenges, an approach which combines solid gospel principles with our modern understandings about human motivations and relationships. Truly effective people, in the absolute sense of these words, are the ones who have learned how to give Christ access to the whole of their life and, in doing so, they have, to coin a well-known phrase, entered the 'space where the "magic" happens'.

I know of no psychological principle which offers power to change and become something better that is able to compare with the old evangelical invitation to 'come to Christ and begin again'. There is no advice obtainable from any other source that has a dynamic comparable to the kind of energy which is released in the personality by what is called the conversion of a soul. The surrender of the whole life to the sway of Jesus Christ; the day-by-day affirmation of renewed loyalty to Him and the fellowship with others who have found what you have found – these things release a power and an energy into human lives that have no parallel elsewhere.

I can only state my conviction, which comes after eighteen years of psychological study and practice and a Christian experience going back much further, that a real experience of Christ, which follows surrender and loyalty to Him, is the most powerful force that the human personality can know and history shows it to have produced the greatest transforming energy our world has ever seen.

Meeting God, Making History and Personal Mastery

A study of both Old and New Testaments shows that godly men and women who lived effective lives all had certain habits of thought and activity in common. First, they all *met God*. They had a personal encounter with Him that changed their lives. They experienced a new beginning which gave them a new life as well as a new perspective on life.

These same men and women went on to make history. Their lives had impact for good and for God in varying ways and to varying degrees.

What enabled them to lead such satisfying and effective lives when others around them did not? Their secret lay in the fact that, after meeting God and before going on to make history, they were able to gain *personal mastery* over themselves and their circumstances. Something was continually going on in their lives that caused them to be open to all that God would do in them and subsequently through them. They were able to recognise and align themselves with the purposes of God for them and their generation. They stood apart from the spirit of the age in which they lived and instead became vehicles for the fulfilment of the Divine purpose and, as a result, better people in themselves.

These same patterns of belief and behaviour continue to manifest themselves in Christ's men and women to this day.

This book is about the thought patterns and life habits of people like this, and they are important because it is the active presence, or absence, of these that will either help or hinder us as we seek to enter into the reality and power of 'the truth' that will not only make us free but make us effective as Christian people at every level of human experience.

'Transformation' not 'Information'

The key purpose of the book is to invite you to examine your faith and life from a fresh perspective with a view to developing your relationship with Jesus Christ and deepening your commitment to His gospel.

The content and structure is designed to be *transformative* rather than *informative*. This is the age of the 'information' society. Knowledge abounds and is increasing day by day. The flow of information appears unstoppable. The need to create it, gather it, analyse it and spread it around has become an integral and, in some cases even necessary, part of everyday life.

Ironically, most of us don't want information pure and simple, as though we were addicted to it; that's not our goal. What we're really looking for is transformation; something that will change our lives for the better.

This book is structured around three major issues:

The first is *knowing yourself*. This knowledge, when it comes, often produces an inward sense of the need for some kind of change in certain key areas such as how you think, what you believe and the way you behave.

The psalmist prayed for self-knowledge when he said, 'Search me, O God, and know my heart; try me and know my anxieties; and see if there is any wicked way in me, and lead me in the way everlasting' (Ps. 139:23–24).

Next is *knowing God*. Four highly significant disciplines are described and illustrated with the help of 'case studies' showing how they are to be pursued. These are the paths to spiritual power and will bring you to the place of effectiveness. 'The people who know their God shall be strong and carry out great exploits' (Dan. 11:32).

Third is *knowing your calling*. It is key that you know what it is that you are called to do and to be and that you stay focused upon that. This is not something that we decide; rather it is something we discern. Possessing discernment of this kind is as important as the disciplines we pursue because it affects the vision we have, the kind of goals we set and the way we fulfil them.

These three concepts – knowing yourself, knowing your God and knowing your calling – are of fundamental importance, and effective living is founded upon them. I've addressed them in a style that is designed to encourage you to engage with the concepts and help you to recognise ways in which you can *own* them personally and begin using them to experience the changes you want and need.

At the end of each chapter there are some suggestions, ideas and questions to provoke your thoughts and stimulate you to take constructive action.

The ultimate goal of the book is to bring you into living, vital contact with the One who transforms lives for His glory, and it will achieve its purpose insofar as it succeeds in reaching that goal.

Reflection

Before going on to the next chapter, take time to reflect on this:

- What is the one thing that you know, if you did it really well and consistently, would have significant positive results in your personal life?
- What is the one thing that you know, if you did it really well and consistently, would have significant positive results in your 'ministry'?
- If you know these things would make such a significant difference, why are you not doing them?

CHAPTER ONE
Fulfilling Life's Purpose
Why Trying Hard is Not Enough

It may be said that there are two important days in the life of every man who has left his mark upon history. There is the day when he was born into the world; and there is the day when he discovers why he was born into the world. (William Barclay)[5]

For I know that in me (that is, in my flesh) nothing good dwells; for to will is present with me, but how to perform what is good I do not find. For the good that I will to do, I do not do; but the evil I will not to do, that I practice. (Rom. 7:18–19)

Philosophers and thinkers, even theologians, tell us that as human beings we are constantly asking ourselves three deep and basic questions: Who am I?; Why am I here?; Where am I going? We are not always aware that we're doing this; sometimes the action is subconscious but it happens nevertheless. These questions come from the roots of our being; they are fundamental to our existence and when they arise within us we find ourselves routinely pressing for answers.

The answers we give ourselves are not always helpful or inspiring as, for example, in these widely quoted lines from Shakespeare:

Life is but a walking shadow, a poor player. That struts and frets his hour upon the stage. And then is heard no more. It is a tale. Told by an idiot, full of sound and fury. Signifying nothing.[6]

Think about this. Do you agree with these sentiments?

There are certainly times when it may feel like a good description of our own human life, but is it true? Of the three questions cited above 'Who am I?' is probably the most important. It has to do with our identity and this matters because everything else about us flows from the answer we give ourselves.

Being, Doing and Having

Life is a matter of *being, doing* and *having,* in that order. Quite often we reverse the order and we think of *having* first. We say, 'If only I *had* this amount of money or those resources, then I could *do* the things I want to do and after that I would *be* the person I want to be.'

We are living life in the wrong order.

It begins with who we are. We do what we do because we are who we are and as a consequence of this we have what we have. We should not try to get our sense of identity or significance from what we do or what we have but from simply knowing who we are. Everything that follows in your life takes its character and gets its motive from that. Your security, sense of self-worth, aspirations and expectations, whether good, bad or indifferent, all come from the belief you have about who you are.

Who Do You Think You Are?

The great apostle Paul said, 'By the grace of God I am what I am, and His grace towards me was not in vain; but I laboured more abundantly than they all' (1 Cor.15:10). He did what he did because he was secure in the knowledge of who he was.

Who do you think you are? What do you believe about yourself? This is important because your behaviour, the activities you engage in and the general direction your life takes mostly come from the beliefs you have about yourself. Whether these beliefs are right or wrong makes no difference.

What gives your life its meaning and purpose? Think of the many roles you fulfil: parent, spouse, teacher, church leader, sports enthusiast. Or what about the clubs and societies you belong to? To what extent does the sense of who you are and the feeling of self-worth that comes with it, derive from these roles you perform or the activities you engage in?

Suppose some of these were to be taken from you, as may happen when you retire or you are no longer required? Some things are perhaps less fulfilling than others and so they matter less to you, but what would be the one thing which, if you were to lose it, would make your life feel empty and flat?

It happens a lot. People who have held key positions in a business or church or a voluntary post in their community often report that when the job comes to an end, or they no longer have the position, they feel 'lost'. It's almost as though they don't know who they are anymore and this feeling continues until they find a suitable replacement for the thing they used to do. Sadly, some never quite manage to do this and for them the consequences can be devastating.

Losing your identity, the sense of who you are, can bring quite serious problems. Self-esteem diminishes. Energy and creativity decrease. Behaviours may change and even become abnormal.

Life begins to run down.

A surprising number of us get our sense of personal identity from the things we do and the things we own. We're not always fully aware that we're doing this, but just pause for a moment and think about it, because this is what makes us vulnerable.

As Christian people we want to be better and more effective across the whole spectrum of life: better spouses and parents; better at our jobs; better in our relationships; more effective in our accomplishments; better in the contribution we make to the life of others and to the life of our churches and to the advancement of Christ's Kingdom everywhere; better in terms of the influence we exert and the usefulness we have within the communities where we live. In short, we want to do and be all that God intends and has made us capable of.

And why not? These are wholesome and perfectly natural aspirations to have. This kind of 'self-realisation' is quite legitimate. But how do we reach this place? This chapter is called 'Fulfilling Life's Purpose' and, whatever that purpose turns out to be for you, the central message is that trying hard is not, by itself, going to get you there!

The Undiscovered Self

The key to realising the things I've just listed, and much more, is for you to recognise who you are in Christ and begin cooperating with the Divine process that is operating in your life to make this a reality.

How do you do this?

In his excellent little booklet *Your Mind Matters*, John Stott, the noted Anglican preacher and teacher, explains two kinds of mental discipline to which we are summoned in the New Testament. The first relates to *self-control*, which is predominantly a matter of controlling the mind because what we dwell upon in our minds will largely determine the kind of person we become – more of this later.

However, there is a second discipline which requires us to consider, not just what we should be but, what by God's grace we already are. Stott says:

> *We are constantly to recall what God has done for us, and to say to ourselves: 'God has united me with Christ in His death and resurrection, and thus obliterated my old life and given me an entirely new life in Christ. He has adopted me into His family and made me His child. He has put His Holy Spirit within me and so made my body His temple. He has also made me His heir and promised me an eternal destiny in heaven. This is what he has done for me and in me. This is what I am in Christ.*[7]

The apostle Paul keeps urging us to 'call these things to mind'. Ten times over in his letters to the Romans and to the Corinthians he utters this incredulous question, 'Don't you know?'[8] 'The reason he keeps asking this over and over,' says Stott, 'is not to ridicule our lack of knowledge or make us feel intellectually deficient. He does it to encourage us to recall these great truths about ourselves and to get us to talk to ourselves about them until they grip our minds and mould our character'.[9]

This is the discipline that is urged upon us and it goes far beyond the self-confident optimism of the positive thinkers whose way is to employ artificial means that get us to pretend we are something other than we are until we become that other something. Paul's way is to remind us of what we truly are, because the grace of God has made us that way in Christ.

Christians are not just nice people who think good thoughts, live clean lives, try to help others as much as they can and try to make sure that their self-talk is always positive and uplifting. These things are good and commendable but Christianity is more than this.

Dr John Baillie (1886–1960), Professor of Divinity at Edinburgh University and Moderator of the Church of Scotland put it succinctly:

> *What makes a man a Christian is not his intellectual acceptance of certain ideas nor his conformity to certain rules but his possession of a certain Spirit and his participation in a certain Life.*[10]

You should know that as a Christian you have within you right now, all you need to bring about the changes you desire personally and also to accomplish the things that God has set out for you to do. This is implied in these words of the apostle Paul: 'We are His workmanship, created in Christ Jesus for good works, which God prepared beforehand that we should walk in them' (Eph. 2:10).

These resources may not be fully developed within you yet but it is important at this stage that you acknowledge their dormant presence. You have the potential and now you must take the next step.

The Neglected Mind

It is not enough to know what we could or even should be; we must go further and set our minds upon being it. The battle is nearly always won in the mind and it's by the renewal of our minds that our character and behaviour become transformed. For this reason the Scriptures also call us to pursue that other discipline, mentioned earlier, which is the mental discipline of self-control. There is an expression, albeit rather quaint, that describes the goal of this discipline precisely and vividly. It is takes the form of a brief but powerful guiding principle: *become who you are.* This also expresses the essence of Christianity; it is the process of 'becoming who we are'.

As well as knowing and being sure of our identity in Christ we also have to live it out and this requires us to use our minds. We must be wary of the menace of mindless Christianity; we are not robots or mediums, we are vessels.[11] What we do takes its character and gets its uniqueness from our personality. This raises an important question. If I am to live authentically as someone who is 'in Christ' does this mean that my capacity to direct my life and exercise freedom of choice is in some way compromised or bound?

What part does the human play in all of this? In a world where God's will initiates everything, does my will only get in the way? If my will is broken, am I still me? Am I complete or do I become an automaton?

The relationship between God's will and my will is not a specialised religious question we should leave for theologians to discuss; it is *the* question for all of us. The way we answer it shapes every facet of our humanity. In a thought-provoking article, 'Growth: An Act of the Will?', Eugene Peterson talks about living in the 'middle voice'. He says:

> *The middle voice is that use of the verb which describes the subject as participating in the results of the action. I do not control the action; that is a pagan concept, putting the gods to work by my incantations or rituals. I am not controlled by the action; that is a Hindu concept in which I slump passively into the impersonal and fated will of gods and goddesses. I enter into the action which was begun by another, my creating and saving Lord, and find myself participating in the results of the action. I neither do it nor have it done to me; I will to participate in what is willed.[12]*

'It's Not About You'

There is a path mapped out for our feet to follow and a purpose for our lives to fulfil and this may not be what we would naturally choose for ourselves; it is 'set before us' (Heb.12:2) and here we must recognise and respect the sovereign will of God over our lives. The opening words of Rick Warren's book *The Purpose Driven Life* are particularly striking. He begins by saying:

> *It's not about you. The purpose of your life is far greater than your own personal fulfilment, your peace of mind or even your happiness.[13]*

We choose what has been chosen for us; we are willing for that which has been willed.

Far from being a limiting experience, this is one which is life-giving and liberating. The words of Christ assure us of this and, at the same time, challenge us: 'Whoever desires to come after Me, let him deny himself, and take up his cross, and follow me. For whoever desires to save his life will lose it, but whoever loses his life for My sake and the gospel's will save it' (Mark 8:34–35).

How much potential do we have? What can we accomplish? What might we become?

Nobody knows! The New Testament urges us to believe that there are no limits: '[He] is able to do exceedingly abundantly above all that we ask or think, according to the power that works in us' (Eph. 3:20).

Why then do some people seem to forge ahead while others hesitate and falter at every hurdle? What is it that keeps us from becoming all that we are meant to be? Clearly there is something in the mix that is having an adverse effect.

We Are Not Where We Hoped to Be

Author and playwright J.M. Barrie wrote:

> *The life of every man is a diary in which he means to write one story and writes another; and his humblest hour is when he compares the volume as it is with what he vowed to make it.*[14]

There are many good people whose standing as Christians is not in any doubt. Their faith is real. They acknowledge the truth of the Scriptures and they have a certain grasp of theology yet somehow they appear to lack the inner strength of character and even the spiritual poise and effectiveness that leads to the kind of accomplishments which the New Testament says are the inevitable result of Christian living.

Their lives seem closely contained and many are trapped in patterns of thought and behaviour that hold them back or even lead them away from their God-given goals and aspirations. They possess habits and attitudes that sometimes lessen their effectiveness as Christians and hinder their spiritual progress. You may even be able to verify this from your own experience or the experience of others around you.

Whatever the causes, one thing is certain: becoming who we are in Christ and going on to realise the full potential of Christ-empowered living are things that do not simply happen to us by default.

It's tempting to blame lack of opportunity or bad luck or the failure of others to help us when we needed help. It's easy to think that circumstances have somehow conspired against us, but one stubborn fact remains and it is this: our greatest challenges do not come from what is going on around us but from what is taking place within us.

Pause here if you will and think about the statement you have just read. Read it again if necessary; the implications are profound.

As you venture out into your own world with great purpose and determination, you will find that your 'inner' life will either help carry you through to success or become the main reason for failure.

The words of Matthew's gospel are startling. Commenting upon the second visit of Christ to his home town of Nazareth, he says: 'Now He did not do many mighty works there because of their unbelief' (Matt. 13:58).

If we were able to probe the reasons for this unbelief we would uncover minds deeply grooved by habitual ways of thinking and behaving over the years; beliefs and attitudes of heart engrained upon the personality plus a whole variety of mindsets that limited the individuals who possessed them.

Barriers to Faith

There are barriers of the mind which can prevent truth reaching our hearts. The mind in itself is not an obstacle to be repressed or ignored. It is the falsehoods that are held in it as truth that need to be abolished and replaced. Our thoughts and perceptions, our beliefs and opinions – whether right, wrong, good or bad – are the things that influence the way we behave and act. They can prevent Christ from having full access to our lives and can become barriers to our growth and development and to the achievement of our God-given potential.

There are also spiritual barriers or blockages which may be caused by a whole range of personal behaviours and practices that can lead to alienation from God, and also by malevolent spiritual activity that is taking place beyond the human stage. These barriers and obstacles need to be dismantled and overcome, and they can be, as later chapters of this book will show. The message of the Scriptures is that with the help of God they can be dealt with and changed so that instead of limiting us they actually liberate us. The often-quoted words of the apostle Paul explain how.

*Be not conformed to this world, but be transformed by the
renewing of your mind, that you may prove what is that good
and acceptable and perfect will of God.* (Rom. 12:2)

What do You See When You Look at Your Life?

Sometimes it's useful to think of society as divided into two kinds
of people. There are those who are 'made *by* the times'. They are
the product of the age in which they live and the society to which
they belong. They have been moulded by its pressures, shaped by
its values and influenced by its cultural and social norms.

Then there is another class of person who might properly
be described as 'made *for* the times'. Dr Martin Luther King Jr
famously described them as 'transformed non-conformists'![15]
I'm not talking about those who happen to be 'movers and
shakers' compared with those who are not. Or who are 'leaders
and innovators' compared with those who are 'followers and
supporters'. The distinction is more significant than that. For
Christians, 'made for the times' has a special meaning. It is not
simply about 'being the best we can be' or attaining some form
of self-actualisation. It is more a matter of living up to, and living
out, everything that God has made us capable of and intends us
to be.

Pause here for a moment and consider which of these
expressions best describes you at this stage of your life: *conformed*
or *transformed*. Instead of being 'conformed', we are to be
'transformed'. The word is 'metamorphosed' and means a change
that takes place from within.

Being conformed implies change caused by constraint and pressure from the outside. It is the kind of change that is imposed upon us.

The lesson is clear. The words of the apostle, quoted earlier and famously translated by J.B. Phillips, spell it out – *'don't let the world squeeze you into its mould'*.[16] We listen to the idle gossip of a friend, follow someone else's lead, fit our lives into a mould that was not of our making and so we are changed by the lives we live. For most of us it is seldom the calamitous change brought about by catastrophic events. It is the slow, sure change of the environment – the change forced upon us by the world around us. What we become part of, becomes part of us. What we perceive and what we accept is an important part of what we will eventually become.

We allow ourselves, in effect, to become moulded by the size and shape of our 'container' which is a world that increasingly seems to want us to believe that its way is the only way. We must break the mould and find that other way if we would begin to live that other life.

The Challenges We Face

In relation to this process of change and development, the Word of God sets out certain key principles of belief and action for us. These are referenced throughout the Scriptures and dealt with fully in the next chapter but the following words, taken from the letter to the Hebrews, give a brief summary of what we should look for in ourselves if we are to live effectively and successfully:

Let us lay aside every weight, and the sin which so easily ensnares us, and let us run with endurance the race that is set before us. (Heb. 12:1)

In the context of being and doing all that God intends, we face three major challenges.

The first of these might be described as the need to get rid of the things that clutter our lives. 'Let us lay aside every weight' (Heb. 12:1). These things are not necessarily sinful in themselves but they hamper us and hold us back in a variety of ways. 'Gird up the loins of your mind,' says the apostle Peter (1 Pet. 1:13) and he is talking about barriers that exist in our minds. We carry a lot of 'baggage'; stuff from our past, the way we've been taught to think, things we've come to accept as true, experiences that have shaped how we look at the world around us, emotional hurts and disturbances that still cause pain, 'hang-ups' we hang onto that even yet continue to influence our attitudes and behaviours, paralysing right action and producing wrong action.

A second challenge is the requirement for us to be radically right with God. 'Lay aside the sin which so easily ensnares us.' This means dealing with the things that contaminate our life. Beliefs we carry in our minds translate into actual behaviours both bad and good.

The third is to follow a life path that is mapped out for us, 'run . . . the race that is set before us'. This means recognising the sovereignty of God and submitting to it.

All three are connected: the first two, 'getting rid of the baggage' and 'getting radically right with God', create a platform for doing the third, finding and following our life path, which is the outward manifestation of a change that has already taken place inwardly.

Private victories always come before public victories and the outcomes envisaged will not manifest themselves in your life unless and until they have first taken place inwardly.

Beliefs and Behaviour

Let's look at the first of these: getting rid of the baggage. It's not a call to declutter your life, tidy your workspace or simplify your lifestyle. Have you ever tidied your garage over a weekend then wondered why it drifted back to being untidy again after two or three weeks? Simply trying hard and being determined to be different is not enough. The issue runs much deeper than that.

What you believe determines how you will behave and act
We all have patterns of thought that crystallise into beliefs and these are what drive our actions and behaviours. Whatever you believe about yourself will end up affecting what you do. Thoughts have a way of gathering with other similar thoughts then, slowly, over a period of time they begin settling in your mind to become beliefs. People sometimes talk about 'living out their own truth'. Your beliefs represent what 'truth' or 'reality' is for you. But this *reality*, which is carried in your mind, is only your perception or your version of the real truth. It may not be accurate, it doesn't have to be. All that is required is for you to believe it and it will be effective for you. This means that most of what 'truth' really is to each of us is based on what we have come to believe, whether true or not.

These beliefs are sometimes called 'guiding fictions' because they are not necessarily 'the truth' but they influence our behaviour and actions nevertheless. You can have beliefs about anything. For example, they can be about the kind of person you are; the opportunities you have, or don't have; the way you are meant to relate with others socially or in a work environment; what you are capable of, or not as the case may be, and you will continue to act according to those beliefs, even though they may be completely untrue, *until you change them*.

Our minds are cluttered with thoughts and beliefs that are wrong, misleading and not helpful to us. To get rid of these and replace them with those that are more appropriate we need to 'be renewed in the spirit of [our] mind' (Eph. 4:23). It's not so much the thoughts and ideas and suggestions that come to us daily that matter; it's the way we think about them and what we do with them that counts.

Our perceptions govern our beliefs and our behaviours

The way we perceive what is going on around us and also our relationship to it is very significant. Most of us think we see the world as it truly is but this is not the case. We see not with our eyes but with our soul. We don't see our 'world' as it actually is, we see it as we are; and when we begin to describe what we see, we are, in effect, describing ourselves, our perception.

This doesn't mean there are no absolute truths but it highlights the fact that most of us are not on a quest to find 'the truth' as much as we are looking for evidence that supports a point of view or perception we already have. For example, supposing someone warns you to watch out for a certain person in your church or neighbourhood, telling you that this person is a troublemaker, always looking for confrontation and can be very awkward. If you accept that as 'the truth' then when you come across this person you'll not look for the good in them; instead you'll find yourself watching out for the tell-tale signs which confirm that your newly found belief about them is accurate!

I heard about someone who was travelling to a particular venue one Sunday morning on the New York subway. The carriage was quiet until the train stopped at a station and a man accompanied by three young children entered. The man sat down but the children did not. Instead they ran up and down the carriage and behaved in a noisy, disruptive way, much to the annoyance of other travellers. The man with the children seemed oblivious to their behaviour and simply sat staring at the floor of the carriage.

Eventually the person telling the story got up and asked the man, 'Are these your children?'

The man sat up suddenly. 'Uh, yeah,' he said absently, 'I guess so.'

'Then would you mind keeping them under control,' said the other. 'Their behaviour is annoying the rest of us and it's unnecessary.'

'Oh yes, of course,' said the man, 'I'm so sorry. We've just come from hospital. My wife has just died. The kids have lost their mum and I don't know what to do.'

The person telling the story said, 'In that instant my perception changed and my attitude shifted from wanting to chastise that man and put him in his place, to wanting to do whatever I could to help him.'[17]

There comes a time in each of our lives when we recognise that making progress depends on us recognising that we're going to have to change the way we see other people and the things around us, and that means changing the way we see ourselves.

Perhaps that time is now.

This is not as straightforward as you might think. The apostle Paul throws light upon the activity of powerful spiritual forces that are constantly working to keep us from perceiving absolute truths and also on the motive behind this work:

> *The god of this age has blinded [the minds of them] who do not believe, lest the light of the gospel of the glory of Christ, who is the image of God, should shine on them.* (2 Cor. 4:4)

You have a lot to offer but it is highly likely that right now you are not even coming close to what you are capable of doing or being. You may be trapped by your own system of beliefs and some of the ways in which your past experiences have conditioned you may be what is limiting you right now. This gives a whole new meaning to the words of Jesus, 'You shall know the truth and the truth shall make you free' (John 8:31–32).

What we believe gives birth to what we expect

Your expectations are what you currently see as being possible for you or are likely to happen for you both now and in the future. These may not always take the form of great and lofty aspirations; they can be quite ordinary and may only reflect the way you think things are going to turn out for you in the future. They may also be quite negative so that you are fearful and pessimistic about certain aspects of your life and it's astonishing how often things turn out the way we thought they would! Have you ever caught yourself saying, 'I knew that would happen'?

As a boy growing up I remember being systematically and deliberately told that I'd never amount to anything because people with my background and upbringing never did. I came to believe that as 'the truth' and for many years a kind of self-fulfilling prophecy operated in my life. Things I dreamed about being or doing I dismissed immediately from my thinking believing they were not possible for me. Things I thought would be good for me I turned away from, believing they were not right for me or that I was somehow unworthy or undeserving of them. These are barriers that exist in the mind and they are created by beliefs we have and they are effective.

William Carey, known as the 'father of modern missions' was an English Baptist missionary to India. He had a motto which summed up his philosophy and which also shows that the nature and scope of what we set out to accomplish, whether great or small, is directly linked to the strength of the belief we have about it being possible for us to achieve it. His motto was: 'Attempt great things for God: expect great things from God.'[18]

Carey's motto reminds us that the greatness or littleness of what we attempt is correlated with the greatness or littleness of what we expect and, further, that it is our beliefs that bring us success or failure.

For the Christian, it is the source and justification of these beliefs that matter. They neither originate from us nor reside in us (Ps. 62:5). Our belief is in a God who not only can, but will do things for us and through us. This belief is not an abstract concept that we construct in our mind but a dynamic force that drives us to act and it is expressed quite clearly in the words of the apostle Paul: 'I can do all things through Christ who strengthens me' (Phil. 4:13).

Our beliefs generate habits and attitudes

The beliefs we have at present generate specific patterns of thought and cause us to habitually act and react in fairly predictable ways. You can recognise these patterns of belief and behaviour quite readily and distinguish one type from another.

For example, we develop habits – lots of them. Habits are patterns of behaviour that are formed through repeatedly doing the same thing over a period of time. Your habits develop from the beliefs you hold and they are important. Once a habit is formed you don't have to think about how to do something in order to do it, for example when driving a car or riding a bicycle. Nor do you have to remind yourself or even force yourself to do something; it's something you do naturally. A habit is an instinctive response causing you to act in a certain way under certain conditions and it's driven by a belief that you have.

Habits enable you to act according to your beliefs effortlessly and in that sense they can make you very efficient, but that doesn't mean that you are always very effective. There's a big difference between effectiveness and efficiency: efficient people do things right but effective people do the right things. Practice does not necessarily make perfect but it always makes permanent!

The effect of habits is to keep us acting and behaving the way we believe we should but there is a downside. Your habits may not always serve the purposes you are trying to fulfil. You'll notice this when you want to try something new or different and the old habit seems to keep getting in the way. That's when you realise that your good habit has become a trap. It's a classic case of not being able to see the bars of the cage that imprison you, until you try to get out!

The words of the Old Testament prophet Hosea speak into our lives today:

Break up your fallow ground, for it is time to seek the Lord, till He comes and rains righteousness on you. (Hos. 10:12)

There are habits of life that may prevent or hinder the work of the Holy Spirit as He brings the Word of God to bear upon our lives as seed that is sown. For example, laziness, shallow thinking, selfishness, even 'busyness' are habits that must be broken and replaced by the kind that open us up to His ministry.

On a more positive note, take the case of Daniel, the politician prophet and man of God. He operated at the very highest level of executive power and administrative authority during the first two great world empires. The record of his life and times reveals him to have a very important habit:

He knelt down on his knees three times that day, and prayed and gave thanks before his God, as was his custom since early days. (Dan. 6:10)

Alongside our habits we have attitudes. Like habits, these are derived from the beliefs we have and they help us to act out those beliefs. Attitudes are often mentioned in the same breath as habits as though they were the same, but of course they are not. Our attitudes are our dispositions; they reveal what we are inclined towards, or away from.

William James, the pioneering American psychologist and philosopher who has been labelled 'the father of modern psychology', made a very perceptive observation about the importance of attitudes:

> *The greatest discovery my generation has made is that people can alter their lives by altering their attitudes of mind.*[19]

We can have attitudes to people, places, things, activities, situations, religions, social trends and so on. Attitudes are created through what we've experienced in the past and, like habits, they are reinforced as we exercise them.

They make themselves known through our moods, our temperament, our willingness or unwillingness and our hesitations, and they can affect how we decide to act at any given moment. The Old Testament prophet Jonah had an attitude problem. As far as we can see he didn't have any bad habits but he did have a wrong attitude and it was this that kept him from aligning himself with the plan of God for the people of Nineveh and also for himself (Jonah 1 – 4). Even godly people, servants of God no less, can carry bad attitudes that do not serve the purpose of God and which hinder their own progress and prove a distraction to them.

The value of values

Values are the standards we stick to in all that we do. What are your 'sticking points'? What would you not do no matter what? These days we often hear about 'red lines' being drawn, particularly where negotiations are taking place or deals are being struck. These are the lines that the parties involved vow never to cross. Where are the 'red lines' drawn in your life?

Eric Liddell, nicknamed 'The Flying Scotsman', was the son of Scottish missionaries to China. At the 1924 Olympic Games he forfeited the chance to win a gold medal when he dropped out of the final of the 100-yard race because it was scheduled to take place on a Sunday. His goal was to win gold but not at the expense of a personal value which he prized. Of far greater significance than the event itself, is the principle that underpinned Liddell's action and indeed his entire life.

But what things were gain to me, these I have counted loss for Christ. Yet indeed I also count all things loss for the excellence of the knowledge of Christ Jesus my Lord, for whom I have suffered the loss of all things. (Phil. 3:7–8)

Values are our moral compass and they test the integrity of our beliefs and the validity of our goals or aspirations. They challenge our behaviour and make us feel the need to be radically right with ourselves, our fellow men and, most importantly of all, with God Himself.

Often our behaviour, whether in thought, word or deed, is at variance with the values we profess, and when this happens we feel uncomfortable. The words penned by the apostle Paul, given at the head of this chapter, describe this as the common experience of many of us: 'For the good that I will to do, I do not do; but the evil I will not to do, that I practice . . . O wretched man that I am!' (Rom. 7:19,24). Some successfully ignore their inner voice by cauterising their feelings. To quote Paul once more, 'having their own conscience seared with a hot iron' (1 Tim. 4:2). But this solves nothing. Instead it leads to moral darkness, separation from God and a loss of purpose. When what we value is in opposition to the natural laws that govern peace of mind and quality of life, we base our lives upon an illusion and set ourselves up for failure. We cannot be a law unto ourselves.

Laws from heaven for life on earth

Not all the values we possess come from the beliefs we have developed.

Dr Martin Luther King Jr famously remarked during a sermon preached at Detroit's Second Baptist Church, 'Men have added an eleventh commandment to the law of God, "thou shalt not get caught".'[20]

Consider these words:

> For when Gentiles, who do not have the law, by nature do the things in the law, these, although not having the law, are a law to themselves, who show the work of the law written in their hearts, their conscience also bearing witness and between themselves, their thoughts accusing or else excusing them. (Rom. 2:14–15)

The law here alludes to the great moral code of the universe, given by the Creator to govern and guide the actions of humankind. Whether written in tablets of stone in the form of the Ten Commandments or written in the human heart, they express God's absolute standards and come as values that continually monitor and challenge our behaviours and the beliefs that drive them. When our beliefs and behaviours are in conflict with the values that confront us we have a challenge that can only be resolved in one of two ways. Either we override the Divine standard and go our own way, or we change our behaviour. The down-to-earth words of that most practical of New Testament writers, the apostle James, tell us, 'To him who knows to do good and does not do it, to him it is sin' (Jas. 4:17).

The Challenge of Being Radically Right with God

We may deal with the baggage that hampers and clutters our thinking and living and still not address the need we have of being radically right with God. This second challenge means dealing with the toxic waste that contaminates our life.

Sin takes many forms. Sometimes it's in the form of *attitudes* we have, including false pride, unjust anger, bitter envy, malicious hatred.

At other times they take the shape of *specific actions* we indulge in, like getting drunk, committing adultery, stealing or blaspheming.

There are also sins that *occur by default* as when you fail to do things you know God has commanded you to do.

And there are sins we *carry out by intent*. This would be a sin you committed in wish but not in reality. For example, the adultery committed in the heart which Christ described in Matthew 5:28. You're not so much guilty of the act itself, but of the intention to commit it.

Sin is an ever-present danger. It spoils our relationship with God. It represents a leak in our spiritual energy system that will rob us of power and lessen our effectiveness. It will drain us of our spiritual resources, destroy our usefulness and reduce the likelihood of us fulfilling the God-given purpose of our life. We must take it seriously and continually monitor our thoughts, words, actions and behaviours in the light of God's Word and with the help of His Spirit. Where we recognise the presence of sin and the impact it is having upon us then we have to lay it aside by turning from it in repentance and confession.

If we say we have no sin, we deceive ourselves, and the truth is not in us. If we confess our sins, He is faithful and just to forgive us our sin and to cleanse us from all unrighteousness.
(1John 1:8–9)

What kind of a sinner are you?

As you read this you might react by thinking, 'And what kind of a question is that?' But when you're dealing with an issue like sin, it helps to know. As well as being aware of the presence of sin, sometimes you'll notice proneness to a certain kind of sin, the kind that 'so easily ensnares us', and so begin to discern that there's a definite pattern to it; for example, there is the *hardened* sinner. This is the one who is dedicated to evil. They know what they are doing and they want to do it repeatedly; they can't help themselves.

Next there is the *drifting* sinner. These are the ones who sin by default. They don't intend to do evil but nor do they incline themselves to doing God's will. They just keep drifting effortlessly into it.

Finally there is the *struggling* sinner. If you don't fit with either of the first two then you're likely to be of this third kind; wanting to do God's will but struggling to overcome your sinfulness.

Sin is a habit and when we seek to be rid of the habit and be radically right with God it helps if we know the shape and character of what we are dealing with. Whether it be sins of omission or commission, of attitude or imagination, that which starts off being occasional has a way of becoming frequent and frequent has its way of turning into regular and regular eventually becomes constant. It is for you to know the sin or sins that so easily ensnare you and to gauge where you presently are on the continuum of practice in relation to it.

Are you hardened to it, drifting into it or struggling with it? Only you can know this. We must root it out and stop the rot. This is our second major challenge and it is spiritual.

Trying hard will not do it; cooperating with the Divine process unfolding in our lives will.

Your Mindset Matters

We develop core beliefs or basic assumptions about ourselves which not only help define who we believe we are but also of what we believe we can and should do. From these habits and attitudes, values emerge and our expectations of what can be for us take shape. Together they coalesce into a 'mindset' which makes us predisposed to act or respond in a certain way.

We have many different mindsets and not all of them are bad but those that are can act as barriers which stop us from cooperating with the Divine purpose. It is the apostle Paul who reminds us that far from cooperating with God's purpose there is a mindset that actively opposes God and His ways: 'Because the carnal mind is enmity against God; for it is not subject to the law of God, nor indeed can be' (Rom. 8:7).

These obstacles and the conditions they create cannot be overcome simply by trying harder. The practice of making New Year's resolutions and seeing them come to nothing after about three or four weeks shows this!

How many times have you resolved to be different in some way? Perhaps you determined to get up each morning at 6.00 a.m. and read your Bible and pray for an hour, or maybe you decided to change some practice in your life that you knew was causing problems for others as well as yourself. You worked at these things from the best of intentions and tried really hard for a while but then your resolve crumbled, the process proved too exhausting for you and, before you knew it, you'd slipped back into your old ways once more.

What went wrong? Was the goal you set too much for you to achieve? Not at all, you have all the potential you need both to do and to be whatever it takes, remember that.

The old beliefs and attitudes you at present possess are too powerful. They cannot be easily overcome. The habits you have formed, perhaps over years of training, which keep you behaving and functioning the way you do, almost automatically it would seem, are so strong that you can really only override them temporarily. These are the things that need to change and they can be changed!

We should recognise that our mind plays an important part in God's overall scheme and in His plan for us. It is not to be neglected or ignored but it does need to be renewed.

New Minds for Old

The renewed mind is a mind informed by the Word of God and inspired by the Spirit of God and has to be distinguished from the mind of the flesh which is 'enmity against God' (Rom. 8:7) and which gets its inspiration from sources other than God and causes us to behave and act independently of God. The renewed mind senses the mind of God and chooses to act in accordance with it (1 Cor. 2:11–16) and is the key that alone can unlock the door to personal effectiveness and lasting change of the right kind. Paul, in fact, goes as far as describing it as 'the mind of Christ'.

This process of renewal is not primarily psychological, driven, for example, by some kind of cognitive behaviour therapy or the like. Nor is it a process or technique of using the mind simply to create a *better you*; a psychologically well adjusted, more emotionally stable you. It is not a matter of tutoring or educating the mind to develop greater mental efficiency or acquire a cleaner, healthier, more positive mindset. All these things are good and commendable and should not be dismissed or despised, but the renewal of the mind is a process of spiritual refurbishment that involves more than simply changing the things we think about. It represents a fundamental shift in the *way* we think and affects the apparatus of our mind and the way we use it. The result is a mind that becomes the vehicle for the kind of transformation Paul the apostle tells us we need. If we are to find and fulfil the unique and specific purpose of God for us, then our mind has to be renewed.

Effective Christians possess a mind that has been renewed by the Spirit of God according to the Word of God and that is what enables them to cooperate with the purpose and plan of God. Beliefs, together with the habits and attitudes that go with them, and the values that support and validate them, do not become obsolete concepts; quite the reverse. They continue to function and the tremendous energy they release because of the way in which they have been changed, carry us forward in the right direction

Effective Christians also possess a heart that is right with God and a way of life that is daily being cleansed and freed from the power and consequences of sin through the blood of Christ. They have a relationship with God that is authentic – it is real and genuine – and it's valid; it really works.

Lastly, effective Christians are not controlled by what is taking place in their lives. Nor do they control it. They are spiritually attuned to that which is willed for them. They are willing for this and choose to participate in the action.

If we are to fulfil our life's purpose our need is not for greater resolve or more will-power but for a change that is brought about from within us by the Spirit of God through the Word of God.

In the chapters that follow we'll look at how this inner change takes place and how it is maintained.

Reflection

Take some time to reflect on the following:

- What would you do if you knew you could not fail?
- What beliefs do you have that limit you?
- Where in the past have you been unable to take advantage of an opportunity that came your way because a habit or an attitude prevented you?
- Where do you hold back from doing something or going somewhere because it puts you in a situation where you feel uncomfortable?

CHAPTER TWO
'Spirit' and 'Word'
God's Formula for Change, Growth and Spiritual Development

The wind blows where it wishes, and you hear the sound of it, but cannot tell where it comes from and where it goes. So is everyone who is born of the Spirit. (John 3:8)

Our task is not to direct the wind; it is to hoist our sail to catch it. (Anon.)

Who's in Charge?

Who or what is in control of your life? Is it you or does it lie somewhere outside of you with something or someone else? Your idea of where this 'control centre' is located reflects the degree to which you feel you have control over the events and circumstances that impact your life.

Those who believe in self-reliance or self-centred accountability could be said to have an internal control centre. On the other hand, those who feel victimised or not accountable for events profess an external control centre.

It's easy to think that the control is mostly outside of us. Especially at those times when we feel at the mercy of circumstances or when other people and the things they do seem to be what is causing our problems. We talk about 'good luck' and 'back luck' or that life has given us a 'raw deal', as though we're being controlled from outside of ourselves.

The truth is, we have more control over what is taking place in our lives than we are sometimes able to recognise. You may find this hard to accept but at least allow it to jolt you into asking, 'Where is the place of control in my life? Is it outside of me or does it lie within me?'

It is sometimes said that 'every man is the accumulation of his own choices'. Put more simply this means that each one of us is, to a great extent, the person we have chosen to be. This can be a provocative and at times disagreeable notion because things happen to us that seem to be outside our control. We feel we have to accept the outcomes and our lives do change as a result. There are times when the pressure of circumstances is so great that we appear to have little option but to conform. Sometimes we find ourselves in situations where we are extremely vulnerable and we're left feeling we have no choice but to obey.

If we continue to see things this way the chances are that we will develop the mindset of a victim and join the ranks of those who believe that their control centre is more external to them than internal and whose mantra is 'the answer to my problem is for somebody else to do something'.

As human beings we cannot give up accountability for our actions. No matter how pressured we are or how vulnerable we feel the fact remains we are ultimately responsible for the choices we make and for the way we choose to live.

As a boy growing up in Glasgow during the 1950s, I witnessed one of the largest social experiments of its kind taking place at that time. In the aftermath of World War II significant numbers of people were living in abject poverty. Overcrowded, insanitary living conditions were a breeding ground for disease, disorder and violence. In an attempt to improve the lot of ordinary working people it was resolved to rehouse them in four massive new housing schemes to be built around the outskirts of the city.

Around 120,000 people were subsequently rehomed in these new dwellings which had all 'mod cons': bathrooms, inside toilets, plenty of living space, and so on. Within two years conditions on these estates had deteriorated and living standards dropped as tenants returned to the old ways.

Years after, an insightful and well-written article entitled 'Overspill Policy and the Glasgow Slum Clearances Project' appeared in a research journal.[21] It explored the rationale behind the project, highlighted the learning points and drew several conclusions. Towards the end of the article the writer made this observation:

While it is undoubtedly true that accommodation in the peripheral schemes was far better and more sanitary than slum dwellings, the social problems that existed in the slums seemed to follow the tenants out to the new estates. As the gloss rapidly wore off, unemployment, gang violence and poverty once again emerged so that for many people, the only thing that had changed in their lives was their location.

This is a shrewd observation and it underscores the fact that change which is imposed upon us seldom lasts. But it raises other, more fundamental questions such as:

- Why do we live the way we do? Is it because we have no choice or is it because we have chosen, albeit unwittingly, to live like this?
- Why do we become slaves to habits that don't help us or serve us? Why do we keep going back to our 'old ways'?

We live in a society that in many respects is in slavery. Freedom is on everyone's lips; it is announced and celebrated but there are not many who feel free or act freely. The apostle Paul reminds Christian believers of a truth that has a significant bearing upon their lives.

You were slaves of sin, yet you obeyed from the heart that form of doctrine to which you were delivered. And . . . you became slaves of righteousness. (Rom. 6:17–18)

Before we became Christians, because of what we were in ourselves by nature we felt a compulsion to live and act independently of God and to obey instead the dictates of him who is described as 'the ruler of this world' and 'the god of this age' –Satan himself. We had a choice, of course, but it was always a sinful choice.

Now the place of control has shifted, from Satan to Christ.

You have no obligation to do what your sinful nature urges you to do. For if you live by its dictates, you will die. But if through the power of the Spirit you put to death the deeds of your sinful nature, you will live. (Rom. 8:12–13 NLT)

We have a new choice, we can live differently. The place from which our life is to be controlled need not be external. Nor is it just within ourselves, as simply internal. It is to be 'in Christ'; He is our 'control centre'. The clue to obtaining and living the kind of life we want and need does not lie in taking back control for ourselves and becoming self-centred or self-reliant but in becoming 'Christ-centred' and submitting to His control.

This doesn't just mean having an intellectual grasp of the teachings and doctrines of an historical figure (Jesus); it is much more dynamic than that. The final outcome is vividly described by the apostle Paul:

> *It is no longer I who live, but Christ lives in me; and the life which I now live . . . I live by faith in the Son of God, who loved me and gave Himself for me.* (Gal. 2:20)

This is how we put ourselves in the zone where our life can realise its God-given potential. It's the place where the 'impossible becomes possible'; where the intention of God for us unfolds and becomes reality in our experience. The Holy Spirit is constantly urging us towards this place and showing us how to come under the control of Christ.

The Infallible Word and the Indispensable Spirit

The gradual process of sanctification, the goal of which is to make us like Christ and to fit us for living the life and doing the work that God has called us to do, is described by Paul:

But we all, with unveiled face, beholding as in a mirror the glory of the Lord, are being transformed into the same image from glory to glory just as by the Spirit of the Lord. (2 Cor. 3:18)

This is where the potential is and it is realised and released as we allow Christ to live fully in us and to work fully and uniquely through us. Eugene Peterson has an insightful comment about this. He says:

We don't form our personal spiritual lives out of a random assemblage of favourite texts in combination with individual circumstances; we are formed by the Holy Spirit in accordance with the text of Holy Scripture. God does not put us in charge of forming our personal spiritualities. We grow in accordance with the revealed Word implanted in us by the Spirit. [22]

God's way of causing change, growth and development within us so that we become uniquely capable of being and doing everything He intends is always *by His Spirit through His Word*. This lays an important foundation for the development of the whole of our life in Christ and sets the stage for everything that follows.

Christ did not become a servant so that we could order Him about and we must realise that what God wants from us and what we want from God is not going to be achieved by us doing the same old things and thinking the same old thoughts. Christ likened the work of the Holy Spirit to the blowing of the wind and in this respect our task is not to direct the wind; it is to hoist our sail to catch it.

Through the Word of God, the Spirit of God Leads us to Knowing and Living Christ

The Word of God is the source of truth for the Christian, it is the foundation of every belief we have; not only our spiritual and religious beliefs but those that relate to every part of our life and living as well. We are to be a 'people of the Word' in every sense. As we noted in the previous chapter, our beliefs are very powerful. A 'belief' retains its power even when it is false. If you believe something that isn't true it will continue to influence how you behave and act as long as you keep believing it. Everybody believes in something, and in that sense everybody 'walks by faith', because everybody walks (lives) according to what he or she believes. But if what you believe isn't true, then how you live won't be right.

Sanctify them by Your truth. Your Word is truth. (John 17:17)

These words of Jesus are strong and they reflect His utter confidence in the truth and dependability of Scripture. The path of truth for us begins here, with God's Word. This is the source of truth for the Christian; it is the basis of belief and is the final arbiter in settling all questions. Biblical truth provides the basis on which our beliefs and values are formed and it is from these our behaviours are meant to flow. Doctrine may not be the *measure* of Christian experience but it ought to be its *mould*.

All Scripture is given by inspiration of God, and is profitable for [teaching], for reproof, for correction, for instruction

65

in righteousness, that the man of God may be complete, thoroughly equipped for every good work. (2 Tim. 3:15–17)

The Word of God conditions our thoughts and actions but for this to happen we need to go from having an intellectual understanding of it to experiencing the power of it personally. It's not what you believe *about* God's Word that counts; what you believe *because* of God's Word to you is what matters. Believe God's truth and you will live God's way.

The words of Christ confirm this: 'It is the Spirit who gives life . . . The words that I speak to you are spirit, and they are life' (John 6:63) and the apostle Paul attributes the effectiveness of his ministry and that of his companions to the same Spirit: 'God, who also made us sufficient as ministers of the new covenant, not of the letter but of the Spirit; for the letter kills, but the Spirit gives life' (2 Cor. 3:5–6).

The Word of God, inspired and applied to us by the Spirit of God is the primary means of replacing our old destructive habits and ways with new life-giving ones, and this is key to our total transformation. But we must respond. Believing and receiving truth from God is a choice. It's something we decide to do, not something we feel like doing.

We live in an age of sensation. We think that if we don't feel something then the experience has no reality and therefore there's no point in doing it. But the Scriptures waste little time on the way we feel. In fact they teach us something different: that we can act ourselves into a new way of feeling much quicker than we can feel ourselves into a new way of acting!

Faith is the Biblical Way of Responding to God and His Word

This is not faith in yourself or in a system or technique. We can't decide for ourselves what we would like to believe and then expect God to respond to our 'faith'. The same Spirit who interprets the Word for us inspires us with faith to believe it and act upon it.

People have faith in all sorts of things including their own selves. Some even have faith in the concept of 'Faith' itself, seeing it as the instrument or means by which thoughts may be turned into things, as though we can create reality through what we believe. We can't create reality; we can only respond to it.

Christian faith is founded upon the Word of God and it's focused on a person, Christ the Son of God, and it has to become an ongoing way of life, not an ad hoc activity. 'We walk by faith, not by sight' (2 Cor. 5:7).

As you read this book and learn about the thought patterns and habits of effective people and how these develop, you too may be tempted to put faith in 'faith' or in yourself. But this can turn out to be a 'let down'. Faith can be misplaced as well as misinformed. Remember it is God who 'makes it happen' and our trust must be in Him. 'Faith comes by hearing, and hearing by the Word of God' (Rom. 10:17).

Prayer is the Vehicle by Which We Communicate with God

By this means we seek His will, ask for His help and listen for His voice and all the while we express our faith in Him and His Word

(Heb. 11:6). Like the other two it must become a natural, free-flowing way of life, not a knee-jerk reaction to a crisis (Eph. 6:18).

We cannot cleverly word a prayer in such a way that God must answer it. He is under obligation only to Himself. He will always stay true to Himself and keep His Word and His covenants with mankind. It is not our place to determine what is true or try to persuade God to give in to our will. He is the truth. We are to ask according to His will and desire it above everything else.

The words of Christ to His disciples confirm the work and ministry of the Holy Spirit towards us:

When He, the Spirit of truth, has come, He will guide you into all truth . . . He will glorify Me, for He will take of what is mine and declare it to you. (John 16:13–14)

The Holy Spirit interprets the Word of God for us, inspires our faith and guides us in our prayer. These three – faith, prayer and the Word of God – are key drivers in the Christian's life and are not meant to be performed as matters of religious duty only, or seen as doctrines to be stored in the conscious mind as information. They are to be fashioned into the life to such an extent that they become an integral part of our makeup and function for us as naturally as eating or sleeping or breathing.

When these three are fully present in your life they condition and govern your thinking and create the context in which the thought patterns and habits that make for effectiveness can develop and truly work.

Godly Christian character is forged. This leads to the formation of well-founded beliefs and convictions which, in turn, will fuel your aspirations.

'Resist Not', 'Grieve Not', 'Quench Not'

There is always a danger that we resist the Spirit and the Word He brings: 'You always resist the Holy Spirit; as your fathers did, so do you' (Acts 7:51).

As human beings we have a history of resistance to God's Spirit. This means a determined hostility to His working. It is not always brought about by wilfulness or stubbornness on our part. Sometimes it's the result of spiritual, even intellectual blindness. We just don't see that it's God who is at work carrying out His purpose for us. At other times it can be because we are out of harmony with the movements of the Spirit and this can thwart His work towards us.

Again we might 'grieve' the Spirit: 'Do not grieve the Holy Spirit of God by whom you were sealed for the day of redemption' (Eph. 4:30).

This can happen whenever He is disobeyed or gives some new revelation of Christ that brings no response. The things that grieve the Spirit are described in the Scripture from which this warning comes and should be pondered carefully. The subtlety of sin is that it doesn't feel like sin when you're doing it. It can feel god-like – a replay of the episode in the Garden of Eden when the Tempter said, 'You will not surely die . . . you will be like God' (Gen. 3:4–5). It can be fulfilling and satisfying. King David didn't feel like a sinner when he sent for Bathsheba who was another man's wife; he felt like a lover.

Somewhere along the line, worship and adoration of God recedes and obsession with ourselves moves in.

We may also 'quench' the Spirit: 'Do not quench the Spirit' (1 Thess. 5:19).

This is about His presence with us as a power for service; it describes His work through us to the world. When the Holy Spirit came at Pentecost it was as tongues of fire that rested upon the disciples of Christ.

Quenching the Spirit implies reversing that condition and this is something that we may cause. Wittingly or unwittingly, we can damp the fire down or even put it out by the things we do! Old habits die hard. Old attitudes stay strong. Comfort zones ring-fence our activities.

There are some general guidelines to adopt as we progress and at this stage it is worth noting what these are so that we might find ourselves leaning towards what the Holy Spirit is bringing to us and embrace His work rather than dismissing it.

Theology Must Come Before Psychology

We are not in search of self-knowledge. Modern psychology and biblical theology don't always sit comfortably together. Sometimes it is just the terms that differ. At other times the differences are real but they shed light on each other which can be helpful. However, there are areas where the differences are so serious that we have to conclude that here, the teachings and findings of psychology are at variance with Christianity.

We must recognise these things and proceed carefully as we consider concepts and facts that draw upon albeit well-attested and well-researched studies in the field of cognitive behaviour and the neural sciences.

It helps to understand how we function as human beings but if we rely on psychology alone and our understanding does not take adequate account of how God has put us together and what has gone wrong and what His plan is for putting everything right, then we will not make progress.

For psychology to be 'good' it must be informed and driven by a sound biblical theology. In this scenario it is the servant, never the master.

Christ Must Come before Self

We are not embarking on a self-improvement programme. He is at work in us to restore the Divine design and it is important that our priorities are based on commitment to Christ and the Christian way.

God's Purpose Must Come before Personal Fulfilment

This calls for cooperation with the Divine plan. We are not seeking self-fulfilment. Nor are we motivated by self-interest. Our engagement with God's plan is not conditioned by the principle of 'what's in it for me'.

Your present circumstances don't matter. Right now you should be assured that you have great potential. It is for you to discover where it lies. Perhaps you already have some inkling of what you think it may be but up until now you have downplayed it or maybe even suppressed it for so long that you doubt it's even there.

Whether you recognise it or not, God is already on your case. You will know this for a fact when you feel any sense of dissatisfaction or desire for change. This desire for change, for improvement, doesn't originate in you. It is the beckoning of a Divine finger; the pull of Divine love. It is for you to recognise this when it happens and cooperate with it.

> *O God, when my faith gets overladen with dust, blow it clean with the wind of your Spirit. When my habits of obedience get stiff and rusty, loosen them with the oil of your Spirit. Restore the enthusiasm of my first love for you.*[23]

Reflection

Take some time to quietly reflect on some of the following issues raised in this chapter or, if you like, discuss one or two of them with someone.

- Where have you allowed your actions to be controlled by things external to you?
- What implications does the phrase, 'We have more control over what is taking place in our lives than we sometimes recognise', have for you?
- How might allowing Christ to be 'the centre of control' in your life give you more control over what happens to you?
- Which of these do you mostly do: 'Resist the Spirit', 'Grieve the Spirit', 'Quench the Spirit'? What actions might you take to counter this?

CHAPTER THREE
What's on Your Mind?
Why You Need to Get Rid of the Rubbish

Everyone thinks about changing humanity but no one thinks of changing himself. (Leo Tolstoy)[24]

Seek those things which are above, where Christ is, sitting at the right hand of God. (Col. 3:1)

What place does the mind have in your life as a Christian? How should a Christian think? According to the psalmist we are 'fearfully and wonderfully made' (Ps. 139:14). Does that include our mind?

Created to Think

God made man in His own image and one of the greatest features of the Divine likeness in us is the fact that we are capable of thinking. This fact is established in the Scriptures. For example, the first two chapters of the book of Genesis show us God communicating with man in a way that He does not with animals. He expects the man He has put in the Garden of Eden to cooperate with Him consciously and intelligently and to make rational and moral choices. The same theme continues throughout Scripture: 'Do not be like the horse or like the mule, which have no understanding' (Ps. 32:9). On the other hand, man is said to have 'understanding': 'There is a spirit in man and the breath of the Almighty gives him understanding' (Job 32:8). We are made as rational, thinking beings by an act of God's creation. We are created to think.

Several words are used in the Old and New Testaments when referring to the mind. The Hebrew word for 'heart' (*leb*) is the most important and comprehensive of these and refers to the capability we have to think, exercise willpower and feel emotions. That implies having understanding to perceive, being able to analyse, make reasoned judgements, decide, create and imagine.

Another word sometimes used is 'spirit' (*ruah*). This describes the ability to think and plan and exercise skills.[25] The same word is also used when referring to our conscious thoughts.[26]

The Old Testament prophet Daniel also uses this word to describe a mindset or thought pattern: 'His spirit was hardened in pride' (Dan. 5:20). In this case, Nebuchadnezzar had made up his mind about God.

Another word the Bible uses is 'soul' (*nepes*). In the well-known command of Deuteronomy 6:5, the soul, along with the heart, describes the whole inner being as a thinking, knowing and willing force, which must decide to serve God.[27] 'Soul' describes us from the perspective of the choices we make, and in Deuteronomy 18:6 as a thinking, inquiring being.

So, the mind is that part of us in which thought and perception take place and decisions to do good, evil and the like are made. With our minds we choose to accept God and obey Him, or reject Him and rebel against Him.

The downside is that our minds have been affected by the devastating effects of the Fall. Indeed our mind is said to have been 'darkened'.

In this sense the word 'mind' itself is often used, especially in the New Testament, to describe a way of thinking or understanding that stands in opposition to God.[28] (This refers to the 'mind' of someone who does not know God, refuses to acknowledge God and has a mindset that is hostile to God.[29] Paul, as we noted earlier, says this comes about through the influence of 'the god of this age', who has blinded the minds of unbelievers (2 Cor. 4:4).

The Battle for the Mind

In spite of the fallen-ness of our minds God still commands us to use them. He invites us to think, saying, 'Come now, let us reason together' (Isa. 1:18) and in saying that, He is asking us to use our minds.

The fact that God chooses to reveal Himself to us and try to reach us shows the importance of our minds. Whether He speaks through nature, where His revelation is visualised, or through Scripture, where it's verbalised, or through Christ Himself, where it is both visual and verbal (Heb. 1:1-3), the implication is clear: it is our minds that are being addressed and it is presupposed that those same minds can understand the message

The message of the gospel is addressed to our minds using words. Paul puts it like this:

> *For since, in the wisdom of God, the world through wisdom did not know God, it pleased God through the foolishness of the message preached to save those who believe.* (1 Cor. 1:21)

Although our minds are darkened and our eyes are blind, nevertheless the gospel is still addressed to our minds as God's way of opening eyes and bringing the knowledge of salvation.

Salvation involves the restoration of the Divine image in us and this includes the mind. Paul described converts from paganism as having 'put on the new self, which is being renewed in knowledge in the image of its Creator' (Col. 3:10 NIV) and as being 'renewed in the spirit of your mind' (Eph. 4:23).

This is the 'renewed' or Christian mind: here the regenerate mind of the Christian is described in terms of a correct understanding and acceptance of the things and plans of God. It refers to a renewed way of thinking, has a renewed worldview, is inclined towards God and synchronises with God's will.

A renewed mind is the prerequisite for reaching an understanding of God's will.

Your Mind Matters

In the relationship between God and us, our mind has an important part to play and this should not be underestimated or dismissed out of hand as something that is of marginal significance. While it is true that renewal is necessary, this does not get us out of our responsibility to decide at each point to believe, and keep believing God. That stays with us and we remain accountable for the choices we make. Through the mind, the delicate balance between Divine sovereignty and human responsibility is maintained. God may make the apprehension of his revelation possible, but we must decide to employ our mind to grasp it.

As human beings we have the capacity to look forward, to plan, to have forethought. We do this in our mind and this makes us unique in God's creation. Therefore we need to examine carefully what we think about.

There is a saying found in the Old Testament book of Proverbs which tells us as a man 'thinks in his heart, so is he' (Prov. 23:7). This is a comprehensive, all-encompassing truth and it touches the whole of our being and even affects the condition and circumstances of our lives; the outer conditions of your life will nearly always be found to be a reflection of your inner state. Your mind can be thought of as a garden, which can be wisely and deliberately cultivated or left to run wild; but whether cultivated or neglected it must and it will bring forth what is in it.

'The within is constantly becoming the without,' writes James Allen, author of the classic little book *As a Man Thinketh*. 'From the state of a man's heart proceed the conditions of his life; his thoughts blossom into deeds, and his deeds bear the fruitage of character and destiny.'[30]

There is much truth in this and the question for each of us has to be: where are our thoughts taking us? Towards more of the life we want to leave behind or towards a brighter future in spite of the difficulties life throws at us? Any particular train of thought, if you persist in it, will produce its results in your character and circumstances. Our circumstances don't necessarily *make* us what we are; it is more accurate to say that they *reveal* who we are. The thoughts that have long been secretly fostered in our hearts simply await the opportunity to manifest themselves as real outcomes.

Understanding these things is key to appreciating the truths and principles explained in earlier chapters and to helping you understand how you got here and how you can get to where you need to be with your life. Being aware of how we function as human beings creates a platform for change. A longer variation of Tolstoy's quote given at the head of this chapter, amplifies both the need and the challenge:

> *There can be only one permanent revolution – a moral one; the regeneration of the inner man. How is this revolution to take place? Nobody knows how it will take place in humanity, but every man feels it clearly in himself. And yet in our world everybody thinks of changing humanity, and nobody thinks of changing himself.*

This chapter focuses upon what may be on your mind right now; on how it got there, and why much of it may be classed as 'rubbish' (Phil. 3:7–8) which cannot simply be ignored but must be got rid of.

'Know Your Mind'

Neuroscientists estimate that upwards of 50,000 thoughts go through our minds every day. Where do all these thoughts come from and, more importantly, where do they go? What happens to them? What impact, if any, do they have on us?

The workings of the human mind are extremely complex and to this day we have not, as yet, been able to fathom the full extent of those workings. When considering the workings of our mind, there are several aspects which must be taken into account.

First is the one most people are familiar with, our *conscious* or *reasoning mind* – which discerns, analyses, judges and decides. This is what Paul the apostle is referring to when he says, 'Set your mind on things above' (Col. 3:2). These words imply a conscious, deliberate act on our part to continuously focus our minds upon a specific object. This area of consciousness is often thought of as the 'surface mind'. There are many things that rest upon it or can come into focus if we turn our attention to them; we 'call things to mind' and we become aware of them and fix our attention upon them by an act of will.

One of the dangers of the age in which we live is the danger of superficiality, of dealing with surface things. For example, we may become aware of visible and conscious failure in our lives. We sense it; other people can sometimes see it, too, and we deal with it, or try to. But, of course, it's not always failures that we are aware of, there are successes as well and we plan for more of the same. We might become aware of aspects of our conduct that dishonour God, like attitudes to others, habits, practices and so on, and we try to put these things right at the conscious level.

There may be avenues of thought or practice – habit tracks along which imaginations that are unworthy of Jesus Christ parade themselves and we try to put right these visible evidences of failure, or the conscious pattern of thoughts, and rightly so, but we are very wrong if we think that is enough. The key point to grasp here is that simply dealing with the visible and the conscious is not enough; we must deal with the whole.

Are there, then, depths within my personality which are not visible to me? Are there things going on within me of which I am not aware – and do they matter?

The conscious mind is not the whole of our personality; there are depths in the human mind that are below or beyond the region of consciousness and these deeper parts of our personality must be included in our approach to attaining fullness of life and becoming effective in our living. The purpose of God, and the provision of God for us, concerns the whole man and so we must look at the whole of our mind.

Regions of the Mind

There are several well-known analogies that may be offered in an attempt to explain the various aspects of the human mind. Some are overly simplistic, others are less so.

It is helpful to think of a lighted candle standing in a large, dark room. Imagine that the room is full of objects of different shapes and sizes. Those closest to the candle are clearly visible and they stand out sharply. But there are also things in the room which are at a distance from the light and you can only see them dimly and with difficulty. As you get further from the candle, the brightness of the light decreases until it fades completely into the darkness and you cannot see what is there at all. There *are* things there, of course, but they are not within the realm of your consciousness. If you hold that picture in your mind, you'll begin to get an idea of the levels of consciousness that exist in your mind and of how the conscious levels shade into *subconsciousness* and beyond that into the deep places of the mind known as the *unconscious*.

One of the factors vital to effective living is being aware that these regions and depths of personality exist.

For example, you may be reading this book and it has your full attention, more or less, and you are thinking about what you are reading. You are fully conscious of what you're doing. At the same time, other thoughts and ideas may drift into your consciousness perhaps prompted by what you are reading, or you may remember something and deliberately call it to mind; it wasn't in your conscious mind, but it is now.

Again, you may have reason to try and recall the text of the sermon you heard in church last Sunday. At first you can't remember it because it's sitting just below the surface of your mind but, with a bit of effort on your part, it comes back to you. This is the subconscious area of mind from which we can bring into consciousness memories or impressions *if we want to*.

Have you ever tried to remember someone's name and the harder you tried the more it eluded you? There came a point where you gave up and stopped all conscious effort to remember. But that does not stop the subconscious effort; it continues. You hand over the task of finding the name to the subconscious activity of your mind. Your subconscious mind begins at once to work on the problem and goes round the files of memory until it locates the name. Two hours later the name pops up in your mind! The subconscious mind has found it and projected it into your conscious mind; it was there all along and the activity to find it was going on all the time and you knew nothing about it, consciously! That kind of thing goes on all the time and with all manner of challenges.

However, as you push further away from the immediate moment or consciousness of things around you, you find you are merging into the darkness to things you cannot recall. But they are there, they happened. Beyond this area of decreasing light there are depths of mind containing things you cannot consciously recall. It is an area of accumulation and activity of which we are not aware, but it exists.

To change the analogy, the conscious mind has often been compared to the tip of an iceberg. The part that is under water and therefore invisible, is far larger than the part you can see. The same comparison applies to the subconscious and unconscious depths of mind with their many levels.

This image of the iceberg presents an accurate picture, not only of the existence, but also of the relative powers and importance of these particular regions of the mind.

It is almost impossible to exaggerate the importance of the subconscious and unconscious parts of the human mind. There are two major reasons for this importance.

1. The subconscious and unconscious regions of the mind are important because of what has accumulated there.

Underneath this subconscious layer is the vast deep of the mind called the 'unconscious' or 'depth mind'. In this 'unconscious' are all the memories and impulses which your mind has received from the first moment of conscious life – your personal history, your experiences and all the emotions attached to them are archived here. The depth mind is a vast, comprehensive and complete storehouse. You might very easily say, 'I've forgotten who was preaching last Sunday' or 'I can't remember what the sermon was about' or 'I've forgotten where I put my glasses'. But the truth is that *nothing* is ever really forgotten in the sense of being obliterated from the mind. It merely sinks deeply into the mind so that we can't reach it from the surface.

Once you realise this you may begin to understand how important the depths of the human personality are because of what can and does accumulate there. The depths of the mind are not just filled with good and happy memories. Everything gathers there, from the atmosphere of the world in which we live which so pervades our lives; from the assaults of the devil with his subtle and evil suggestions, and from the energy and activity of the sinful nature within us. From these come an awesome accumulation of every thought, every word, every image, every scene, every emotion whether good, bad or indifferent – and all are gathered in the depths of the mind.

You may recall from your childhood years the story of the recording angel with his slate and pencil; it is an image which is commonly found in the literature of the three major world religions of Judaism, Christianity and Islam. Whether this is to be taken literally or understood symbolically matters little, but it is a powerful image and it reminds us that in a much deeper and profoundly important sense, there is a 'recording angel' whose pen never ceases to write. This pen never scratches, and we never hear it. But everything is written down, in complete silence. For it is a fact, everything we have ever thought or seen or said or done, is recorded in our own nature – somehow.

The importance of these deep regions of the mind lies in what accumulates there. The thought process is complex but essentially everything passes into the unconscious part of your mind. Every conversation you've ever had, every TV programme you've ever watched, every book you've ever read, every experience you've ever had are all archived in the unconscious or depth mind.

But it is not just the experience (the physical event) that is recorded; what you 'feel' about what has happened (the emotional event) is also recorded. Your depth mind, by acting as a storeroom for your past experiences, records not only the event but the feelings that accompanied it as well. These feelings may be physical or emotional or both. For example, when my favourite aunt died I wasn't allowed to go to the funeral but I recall watching as they struggled to carry her coffin through the narrow hallway of our house onto the street (the physical event) and felt desperately sad (an emotional feeling).

Another example might be of someone who heard their parents screaming and shouting at each other (the physical event) and felt very afraid (an emotional feeling) and had difficulty breathing (a physical feeling) because they felt so anxious.

Your depth mind stores all these feelings and the more frequently an event occurs, the more deeply will the traces be engraved on your memory. What is stored there may not be the whole truth or even partly true but it is the 'truth' for you; it is what you have perceived as reality.

Repression
Information and memories that are relevant to your life at the present moment need to be easily accessed, so they get stored where they can be returned to without much effort. However, the depth mind has many levels and some things are pushed so deeply into your mind as to make them inaccessible by conscious thought.

Information gets stored at a deeper level either because the memories are no longer relevant to your present life or because they were so frightening and upsetting at the time that they needed to be repressed.

Repression is not something you consciously choose to do, it happens automatically as part of your mind's self-defence mechanism. When an incident is repressed you can't remember it anymore and it's as though it never happened.

So, you don't remember the dark cupboard you got locked into when somebody played a joke on you. But the feelings that went with the event at that time, whatever they were, will come out because feelings cannot be forgotten even if the event itself is. Feelings are always discharged as behaviour and will continue to be until you have found the event that caused them in the first place.

Until you make the connection between being locked in the cupboard with, say, the unreasonable feeling of annoyance you always get whenever someone plays a joke on another, or the irrational feeling of panic that comes over you at times when you find yourself in a crowded room and you just want to get out, or the sickly fear you feel when you're in a large department store and you can't find the exit, you'll always resort to some form of compensatory behaviour. But make the connection and then you put these things in their proper place – the past – and get on with your life.

2. The second main reason why the hidden depths of the mind are so important is because of what is controlled and produced from there.

The title of this chapter poses a question, 'What's on your mind?' and you might ask, 'To which part or parts of my mind is this referring?' The answer is *every* part. The conscious and unconscious levels of our mind do not work independently of each other nor do they compete one against the other. In fact they work together to perceive the world around us and to store our version or perception of what happened and what we perceive to be the real truth of the matter.

But the importance of the depth mind lies not only in the fact of what has gathered there but, more significantly, in what originates from there. It is almost impossible to exaggerate the importance of the unconscious part of the mind. Physical functions like breathing, circulation, digestion and the like are controlled by it.

Choices we make, which might appear to be the result of an impulse or fancy, are conditioned by it. The unconscious determines many choices we make for which we might not be able to give a conscious reason. You may have found yourself saying at times, 'I don't know why I did that' or, 'I don't know what came over me to have made me say such a thing'. The explanation may lie beneath the surface in the depth of your mind.

Ideas that are first received by the conscious part of the mind, after they have sunk into the unconscious region, continue to affect how we think and act. If the depths of the unconscious are reached and penetrated by an idea, the idea tends to materialise. This shows the tremendous importance, and danger, of the unconscious. Once an idea or suggestion gets past the critical sentry on duty, the unconscious takes hold of it as 'truth' and maintains its hold despite all the efforts of the conscious will. In a later chapter, 'Changing on the Inside: Why You Need to Renew Your Mind', it will be shown that this all-important inward change is not brought about by willpower or techniques of suggestibility, but through the exercise of faith which has little to do with suggestibility. Faith and all that is attained through it comes as a result of receiving and believing the Word of God.

The subconscious and unconscious regions of the mind are not just places full of beautiful memories, there are also wastelands here that are filled with the accumulated refuse of the years which are sources of danger and infection, and these energies of the mind sweep through the personality like rushing rivers which are hard to control by willpower and reason. This is implied, in part at least, by the words of Christ: 'From out of the heart proceed evil thoughts, murders, adulteries, fornications, thefts, false witness, blasphemies' (Matt. 15:19). He could have gone on and said, 'anxieties, jealousies, irritabilities, impurities'. All these things come from within and defile a man.

It's no use just dealing with the stuff that's visible and conscious, we have got to get right down into the depths of the mind, somehow or other. Why are some people continually beset with jealousy? Why are others constantly troubled by anxiety? Why are some people's minds filled with irritations? The apostle James, in his immensely practical epistle, says:

If you have bitter envy and self-seeking in your hearts [depth minds], do not boast and lie against the truth. This wisdom does not descend from above, but is earthly, sensual, demonic. For where envy and self-seeking exist, confusion and every evil thing are there. (Jas. 3:14–16)

Is it possible that the rubbish bin of the unconscious is rotting with the accumulation of the years, and our minds are cluttered with baggage that projects itself in the shape of beliefs, attitudes and habits that hinder us and are unhelpful and often harmful to us and to our development?

One of the lessons psychology can teach us is that there is a vital connection between the subconscious and the invisible, and the conduct that is conscious and visible. We may at times say we're going to do one thing yet we do something quite different in the end and the reason for our conduct may lie in our unconscious which is the truly dominating factor.

There is a humorous little piece of doggerel that describes the subconscious mind, but it has a serious side to it:

I have a little Robot that goes around with me;
I tell him what I'm thinking, I tell him what I see.
I tell my little Robot all my hopes and fears;
He listens and remembers all my joys and tears.
At first, my little Robot followed my command;
But after years of training,
He's gotten out of hand.
He doesn't care what's right or wrong,
Or what is false or true;
No matter what I try now, he tells me what to do! [31]

If you don't control this 'little robot' (your subconscious mind), it will eventually control you.

What Is On Your Mind?

Knowing that the 'truth' which is stored in our minds influences our decisions and actions, even though it may not be the truth, should help us understand what 'being 'radically right with God' and 'getting rid of the rubbish' might mean for us.

The Old Testament prophet Ezekiel describes how in a vision he gained insight into what was going on in the minds of the leaders and key influencers among the people of God.

> *So He brought me to the door of the [Temple] court; and when I looked, there was a hole in the wall. Then He said to me, 'Son of man, dig into the wall'; and when I had dug into the wall, there was a door. And He said to me, 'Go in, and see the wicked abominations which they are doing there.' So I went in and saw, and there – every sort of creeping thing, abominable beasts, and all the idols of the house of Israel, portrayed all around on the walls. And there stood before them seventy men of the elders of the house of Israel, and in their midst stood Jaazaniah the son of Shaphan. Each man had a censer in his hand, and a thick cloud of incense went up. Then He said to me, 'Son of man, have you seen what the elders of the house of Israel do in the dark, every man in the room of his idols? For they say, "The LORD does not see us, the LORD has forsaken the land."'* (Ezek. 8:7–12)

This illustrates the power of the imagination and the emphasis is on how wrong and inappropriate beliefs that are etched upon the walls of the secret chambers of the mind – 'every sort of creeping

LIVE BY DESIGN, NOT BY DEFAULT

thing, abominable beasts, and all the idols of the house of Israel, portrayed all around on the walls' – are producing and driving behaviours that are equally inappropriate and wrong – 'what the elders of the house of Israel do in the dark, every man in the room of his idols'.

We need to 'get rid of this rubbish' and this leads to a third important consideration for the Christian; namely, the need for cleansing in the depth mind.

The Need for Cleansing and Renewal of the Depth Mind

The great cry of the psalmist was 'Cleanse me from secret faults' (Ps. 19:12). The way the conscious and unconscious parts of our mind work together may be described as the *law of the mind* (Rom. 7:21). Christians should remember that there is also:

- *the law of God* (Rom. 7:22) – the great moral code of the universe that is given to govern our behaviour and our relationships.
- *the law of sin and death* (Rom. 7:23) – which works in our members defying the law of God and defeating the law of the mind!
- *the law of the Spirit of life in Christ* (Rom. 8:2) which delivers us (sets us free) from the law of sin and death. This brings into focus the role of God's Holy Spirit in the entire process, together with the influence of the Word of God (Ps. 119:11).

Our challenge is to live according to God's truth and that means growing and developing as the person He means us to be and having proper dreams of the future (1 Cor. 2:9–10).

Is there any way, any agency that can somehow penetrate into the unconscious and deal with the rubbish? The following chapter deals with how this all-important inward change takes place. There is a process open to us that will transform us and enable us to live as the men and women God intends. It is orchestrated by the Spirit of God through the Word of God, but if it is to be effective we must cooperate with it.

This next chapter is about how we do that.

Reflection

Pause and reflect on the following:

- How good are you at controlling your thoughts?
- When strong and limiting emotions surge within you, like anger, anxiety and guilt, can you trace them to an obstacle that may be interfering with a chosen goal?

CHAPTER FOUR
Changing on the Inside
Why You Need to Renew Your Mind

You can't talk your way out of a problem that you've behaved your way into. (Stephen Covey)[32]

How can a young man cleanse his way? By taking heed according to your Word (Ps. 119:9)

It's important to remind ourselves that renewing the mind, in the Christian sense, is not simply a matter of replacing old, worn-out beliefs and habits with new and better ones. Nor is it just about replacing negative thoughts with positive ones. The objective is not merely to develop a positive mental attitude; you can do that without being a Christian. Our goal and the aim of this book is much greater than that.

With a renewed mind we become attuned to God's will and over time find ourselves walking in His ways as they are formed within us through His Word. We develop a mindset that inclines us towards God and His will and not away from it. 'Just as you presented your members as slaves of uncleanness, and of lawlessness . . . so now present your members as instruments of righteousness for holiness' (Rom. 6:19).

The Conversations We Have with Ourselves

You won't always notice it but if you pause and listen to yourself you'll become aware of a dialogue that is going on within you; it's a conversation you are having with yourself and no one else. You're giving yourself a running commentary on what is going on around you – about what you are perceiving, what you are experiencing, what you think and feel about it all – and it seldom stops!

Here are some examples:

'The next time I go into that shop I'm going to . . .'

'I think I'm coming down with a cold, I've got a bad headache . . .'

'I'm not going to wear this suit tonight, it makes me look over-dressed . . .'

'There's no way I'm going to be able to give a talk like that to our group . . .'

'I can't do this; I'm just not the right kind of person for this job . . .'

'I wonder what that telephone message was about. Am I in trouble?'

If you listen to this inner dialogue of yours you might notice something else about it: most of the time its tone is negative. That in itself should give us pause for thought.

If you listen to the conversations that are going on around you between people in the workplace, the community or even the messages that are put out through the media, these too are negative to a significant extent. This may be partly explained by the fact that we live in a fallen world, a view that is reinforced by the way in which the Christian Scriptures constantly seek to counter this negativity through the many exhortations they give us concerning the language we ought to use.

Let your speech always be with grace, seasoned with salt. (Col. 4:6)

Let no corrupt word proceed out of your mouth, but what is good for necessary edification, that it might impart grace to the hearers. (Eph. 4:29)

We are 'wired' to be on the alert for threat, especially when fear is involved. Recall the first recorded words that Adam spoke in the Garden of Eden immediately after the Fall – 'I was afraid' (Gen. 3:10).

Since then, negative things seem to have a stronger influence on our perceptions, beliefs, attitudes and memories than positive things or things of a neutral nature. Indeed some research points out that our negative vocabulary, the words we know and use, is much more richly descriptive than our positive vocabulary; it's easier to give yourself vivid pictures of a negative scenario than a positive one.

Has anything like this ever happened to you? A motorist was driving along on a remote country road late one night when he got a flat tyre. To his dismay he realised he didn't have a jack and, as he looked around, wondering what to do, he saw a light in a distant farmhouse. 'That farmer will probably have a jack,' he said. He trudged for about a mile up to the farmhouse and all the way he was building up a morbid expectation:

I bet he's gone to bed and he'll be annoyed because I've woken him. A lot of these farmers are quite selfish, he'll probably find some excuse for not lending me his jack; he might not even answer the door. If he's a farmer then he'll not want strangers on his land at night. He might even wave a gun at me and warn me off. Well, he'd better not take a shot at me!'

By the time he reached the farmhouse he was in quite a stew. When he knocked on the door the farmer appeared and said, 'Hi, what can I do for you? What do you want?'

'I don't want anything from you,' the man blurted out, 'and you know what you can do with your jack!'

Pause for a moment and consider how often you have conversations with yourself that are like the one just described. If you search around in your mind you may conclude that you do this more often than you realise. For example, when you're thinking back over a meeting you've just had with someone and you start to rehearse some of the things you wish you'd said and the way you'd like to have said them. Or when you are planning to return something you've bought in a shop and you're going back to ask for a refund; on the way you start to imagine the response you get from the shop assistant and you muster your arguments and hear yourself responding to this unreasonable shop assistant in no uncertain terms. All this before you've even arrived!

Humorous it may be, but it has a serious side. This kind of thing, if persisted in, can lead us away from the path of faith and lessen our expectation of a good outcome no matter how hard we pray. A sarcastic attitude and a cynical view of the world might appear smart, even justified at times, but it can bring consequences that cascade through everything we attempt to do.

In the previous chapter we saw that we are constantly being bombarded with thoughts, suggestions, ideas and opinions that we initially perceive, through our senses, as information. Much of it is fast and fleeting and there's a lot of it we don't catch, but it happens nevertheless and we feel the impact of it. When new information reaches us, whatever shape or form it's in, we begin to categorise it in relation to what we already know and have decided is right or wrong, good or bad, agreeable or disagreeable, relevant or not relevant, until a point is reached where this flow of information simply gets streamed so that it confirms and strengthens our existing views and opinions.

This 'information' comes from three major sources: first there is *the human spirit*: our family, friends, workmates, people who are important to us, authority figures like educators or ministers of religion or bosses at work, who may be giving out their views and opinions, and these reach us either directly or indirectly, and when they do we instinctively find ourselves agreeing, disagreeing or dismissing the matter altogether.

However, Christians also believe that beyond the 'mind-body' relationship there exists an unseen, all powerful spiritual realm that cannot be ignored or factored out and so a further source is *the Holy Spirit* who speaks to us to inspire us, guide us and instruct us through the Word of God.

Finally, there is *the satanic spirit* who is constantly trying, in a variety of ways, to deceive us, mislead us, misrepresent God and lead us away from Him and His ways for us.

Who Should We Listen To?

There are both negative and positive influences at work in human life. As Christians we have the power to choose who we listen to and what we do with what we hear. It is important that we choose to listen to the 'right' voice. Speaking of a good shepherd, Christ tells us that, 'When he brings out his own sheep, he goes before them; and the sheep follow him, for they know his voice. Yet they will by no means follow a stranger, but will flee from him, for they do not know the voice of strangers' (John 10:4–5).

We need to be aware of negative people and influences who can project their 'truth' on to us. This is not always easy. There are times when we are especially vulnerable and susceptible to the influence and words of others. For example, when you are a child listening to a teacher or a parent. There are many 'authority figures' that appear in our lives from time to time.

Think of some who may be featuring prominently in your own life right now and as you listen to them you may almost feel duty bound to accept what they are telling you; maybe a parent, teachers at school or college, a boss at work, a church leader, a trusted friend, a doctor.

We must be careful who and what we listen to and what we accept as the 'truth'. The voices of past experience, public opinion and common sense all call loudly for our attention and we have the job of discerning between the voices of the human spirit, the satanic spirit and the Holy Spirit. Once we decide what the 'truth' is, it becomes part of us and then all our energy and creativity goes into making it reality in our daily experience.

Dr Martyn Lloyd-Jones in his excellent book entitled *Spiritual Depression* says, 'Have you realised that most of your unhappiness in life is due to the fact that you are listening to yourself instead of talking to yourself?'[33] He goes on to draw an important distinction between listening to yourself and talking to yourself. He cites the words of the psalmist as an example: 'Why are you cast down, O my soul? And why are you disquieted within me?' (Ps. 42:5). This is 'listening to yourself' and it implies dwelling on the doubts and fears that crowd in upon us continually. 'Hope in God, for I shall yet praise Him for the help of His countenance.' This is 'talking to yourself' and implies taking the truth of God's Word and applying it to yourself.

When Adam and Eve were approached by Satan in the Garden of Eden they clearly knew the Word of God for them. Eve confirmed this: when confronted by the Tempter she uttered these words: 'God has said'.[34] But she also listened to the voice and words of Satan and was persuaded by them and this became for her the 'truth' which she later acted upon, and that scenario and others like it have been played out on the human stage from that day until now in every life with disastrous consequences.

In contrast to this, Christ, when He was tempted, responded at every stage of the process with the words, 'It is written'.[35]

From what source are you mostly getting that version of the truth that shapes the way you see yourself and governing your life? Frank Buchman, founder of the Moral Rearmament movement, was a man who mixed with presidents, kings and statesmen in the course of his ministry. A European Cabinet minister came to see him. During their conversation Frank Buchman told him that the only way to answer the needs of nations was by a change in men. He repeated the words of the late Lord Salisbury who said in the House of Lords, 'What we need are God-guided personalities, to make God-guided nationalities, to make a new world.' Soon after this on 7th August 1961, as he lay dying, Buchman uttered these words, 'I want to see the world governed by men governed by God. Why not let God run the whole world?'[36]

These are very perceptive observations. Wise decision making and right action comes through those whose thinking and perceptions are shaped by God. This is also true for ordinary folk like us as we try to be salt and light as well as sources of guidance and pressure in our world.

Ponder the response of the people who listened to Paul and Silas preaching the word of Christ in their synagogue. It is enlightening:

They received the word with all readiness, and searched the Scriptures daily to find out whether these things were so. (Acts 17:11)

If these things are so and represent 'the truth' as it is in Jesus, then we ought to take steps to make them part of our 'inner dialogue'.

Study Your Story

The conversation that is constantly going on within us is crucial because it eventually translates into a series of short stories or scripts that are personal to us, and we don't have just one script, we have thousands of them! We have scripts that cover just about every aspect of our own lives as well as that of other people and of the things around us. These pass into our depth mind, which doesn't question whether they are right or wrong, true or false, good or bad; it just accepts what we give it and stores them as our version of 'the truth'.

These scripts portray and describe the kind of person we think we are – happy, outgoing, bright, intelligent, stupid, unloved, useless, forgetful – the list goes on. They are not just about who we are; they also describe, even define, our capabilities and preferences; our likes and dislikes such as what we do and how well we do it; what we can't do or what we're not good at; what we're like as parents, spouses, work colleagues, church members.

Our behaviour and actions are scripted. Our actions, and reactions, may seem at times to be random or spontaneous but in fact they are not; we are acting in accordance with the script or scripts *that we ourselves have created*. Joseph Locke, one of the founders of the British School of Psychology, spoke about 'the scene of ideas' as though we were watching a scenario unfolding in which a group of actors were playing their respective parts. In fact, we are not simply observing the action, we are 'on stage' and we experience ourselves participating in the action and this is very powerful. Regardless of the scenario, we never forget the appropriate script; we always act it out faithfully whenever and wherever we are called upon to do so. Some of our scripts are good; many of them are not and need to be rewritten.

Norman Vincent Peale tells a story in one of his books about an incident that took place while he was travelling in Hong Kong. Walking through the narrow streets of Kowloon he came across a tattoo parlour run by an elderly Chinaman. In the window of his shop there were displayed various 'decorations' that could be imprinted on your skin if that appealed to you: flags and patriotic slogans, daggers, skulls and crossbones, mermaids, and so on. But the one that caught his eye was the sombre phrase 'Born to Lose'.

This interested him so much that he went into the shop and asked the proprietor if he spoke English. This he did to some extent and so Peale went on to ask him about the 'Born to Lose' tattoo. Did people really want to have something like that imprinted permanently on themselves?

Yes, he said, occasionally they did. The last customer who wanted it had had it emblazoned across his chest!

'Why on earth,' asked Peale, 'would anyone want to be branded with a gloomy slogan like that?'

The old Chinese man gave an oriental shrug. 'Before tattoo on chest,' he said, 'tattoo on mind.'[37]

How true and yet how sad. The born loser was not born that way at all but if he allows feelings of guilt and fear to take hold of his mind, if he continues to accept the statements and negative opinions others make of him (especially if he sees them as authority figures important to him), then over time an impression will form within him that this is the kind of person he is and he'll go out and find ways to 'fulfil the prophecy'.

He will not go and try to prove that he is wrong to believe this; on the contrary, he will try to prove that his belief is correct. He will not allow himself to see or hear or think of anything that might suggest otherwise. He will look only for evidence that supports that view and he will find it and, when he does, it will reinforce the belief he already has.

Where did we get these scripts from? How are they created? Some are simple, brief and very direct. Others are longer and more complex but all of them, without exception, are formed like islands in the stream, out of the flow of the conversation we are continually having with ourselves. Controlling your inner dialogue may be the most important thing you ever learn to do. It affects every belief and every behaviour that plays itself out in your life. Listen carefully to the advice the wise man gives in the book of Proverbs:

> *Guard your heart above all else, for it determines the course of your life.* (Prov. 4:23 NLT)

Watch Out for 'Gate Crashers' and 'Trojan Horses'

You must carefully examine the nature of the things you are continually being confronted with and what you are telling yourself about them. There's no such thing as a neutral thought; we attach a value to everything we perceive and make a judgement about it regardless of how trivial or insignificant it may seem. You must decide what to accept and what to reject and this is not always easy, especially if the source represents an authority figure in your world (Acts 17:11). Whatever you decide the truth is becomes part of you and will eventually gain power in your life, one way or another, and will influence your actions.

Thoughts can be introduced to your mind through your own carnal human spirit or by the satanic spirit as well as by the Holy Spirit, and they can take many different forms. Some are hugely attractive and highly persuasive and can come crashing through our intellectual and spiritual defences to dominate our thinking by taking centre stage.

Others gain entry by a more subtle route. The Trojan horse is a story from the Trojan War about the subterfuge the Greeks used to enter the independent city of Troy and win the war. After a fruitless ten-year siege of the city, the Greeks constructed a huge wooden horse and hid a select force of men inside and left it outside the city. Then they pretended to sail away and the Trojans pulled the horse into their city as a victory trophy. That night the Greek force slipped out of the horse and opened the gates for the rest of the Greek army which had sailed back under cover of darkness. The Greeks entered and destroyed the city, ending the war.

Since then a 'Trojan horse' has come to mean any trick or strategy that causes a target to invite a foe into a securely guarded place. It is something that looks good but in truth has another purpose, usually bad. The story of Adam and Eve being confronted by Satan in the guise of a serpent (Gen. 3:1) is a case in point. The serpent symbolises something both fascinating and loathsome yet neither Adam nor Eve saw the danger embodied in it. Indeed Eve showed no surprise in hearing a strange voice from the snake. The apostle Paul comments on this much later, saying, 'I fear, lest somehow, as the serpent deceived Eve by his craftiness, so your minds may be corrupted from the simplicity that is in

Christ . . . And no wonder! For Satan himself transforms himself into an angel of light' (2 Cor. 11:3,14).

There are thoughts and ideas, suggestions, beliefs, opinions, experiences that can present themselves to us and appear to be sweet and reasonable, harmless, wholesome, even good for us, and yet if we take them in we will find that they contain the seeds of our destruction.

Any thought or idea that you consider might be good for you, if you take it in and ruminate upon it, you will eventually act on it.

The first step towards 'guarding your heart' is to apprehend every thought as soon as it steps through the door of your mind.

Once you have halted a penetrating thought, the next step is to evaluate it on the basis of Paul's eightfold criterion for what we should think about.

Whatever things are true, whatever things are noble, whatever things are just, whatever things are pure, whatever things are lovely, whatever things are of good report, if there is any virtue, and if there is anything praiseworthy – meditate on these things. (Phil. 4:8)

Ask yourself: 'How does this align with God's truth? Is it suggesting that I do something honourable or right or pure? If this thought becomes action, will the outcome be lovely and contribute to excellence in my life? Will other believers approve of my actions? Is it something for which I can praise God?'

If the answer to any of those questions is 'no' then dismiss that thought immediately. Don't have anything more to do with it. If it keeps coming back, keep saying 'no'. When you learn to respond to tempting thoughts by stopping them at the door of your mind, evaluating them on the basis of God's Word, and dismissing those which fail the test, you have found the way of escape that God's Word promises (1 Cor. 10:13).

In contrast, if a thought enters your mind and it passes the Philippians 4:8 test of truth, honour, righteousness, and so on, then let your mind dwell on these things and practise these things 'and the God of peace shall be with you' (Phil. 4:9). This will produce an infinitely better outcome than the pain and turmoil which follows when we yield to tempting thoughts and become involved in sinful behaviour.

Prevention is better than cure but being 'renewed in the spirit of our mind' (Eph. 4:23) refers not only to how we use our mind to correctly censor what we allow to enter it but also how we deal with what has already entered it and needs to be got rid of. For many of us, the majority of our beliefs were formed before we became Christians; therefore it's easy to see why many of our actions do not reflect Christ's character. Until these false beliefs are recognised, ruthlessly rooted out and replaced with biblical convictions, our lives will continue to be filled with destructive thoughts and actions.

We form 'basic assumptions', foundation or core beliefs about ourselves. For example:

'I am a secure, dynamic person. I'll always forge ahead.'
'I am worthless, I'll never amount to anything much.'
'I believe in God.'
'I don't believe there is a God.'

These basic assumptions have been learned through our environment, experience and education and are sometimes called 'guiding fictions' because they guide our lives but may not be true. In extreme cases they can lead to what the Scriptures call 'strongholds' (2 Cor. 10:3–5). Strongholds, or fortresses, are negative patterns of thought that are burned into the mind either through repetition over time or 'one-time' traumatic experiences. Thoughts determine behaviour and thought patterns determine temperaments.

Strongholds are revealed in unchristian temperaments and behaviour patterns. These need to be dismantled, destroyed and replaced by new, more appropriate 'basic assumptions' (Rom. 12:2). The apostle Paul reminds us, 'God has not given us a spirit of fear, but of power and of love and of a sound mind' (2 Tim. 1:7). It is necessary first to expose our root emotions and the false beliefs that are triggering them. Then, by faith, we can allow God's Word to renew our minds.

Here are four common false beliefs:

a. *I must meet certain standards to feel good about myself.*
b. *I must be approved by certain others to feel good about myself.*
c. *Those who fail (including myself) are unworthy of love and deserve to be blamed and condemned.*
d. *I am what I am; I cannot change; I am hopeless.*

The following statements are associated with these false beliefs:

1. *I'll never be a successful spouse and parent.*
2. *I'm so undisciplined, I'll never achieve anything.*

3. *I just can't trust God.*
4. *My father never accepted me.*
5. *This is just the way I am.*
6. *Everything I do goes wrong.*
7. *I can't overcome a particular sin.*
8. *I deserve all the misery I'm experiencing.*

Can you match the statements with the beliefs?
Compare your responses with these:
1. goes with (a) and (d)
2. goes with (a) and (d)
3. goes with (d)
4. goes with (b)
5. goes with (d)
6. goes with (a)
7. goes with (d)
8. goes with (c)

Look at these results again and analyse the issues that lie at the root of each one.

The Golden Rule for Cleansing and Renewing the Mind

Whether it be changing or improving habits, attitudes, behaviours or actions, as a matter of principle we must stand firmly upon the truth of God's Word. Changing your 'self-talk', so called, by rewriting your own personal script may make you a *different* person but not necessarily a *better* person and it will certainly not produce the transformation promised in the Scriptures unless it is the product of a renewed mind.

You may find you have simply exchanged one form of slavery for another, or replaced one fictitious belief with another.

The objective is not simply to 'build a better you'. On the question of the Christian's 'self-image', the Scriptures are clear about what we are to become and who we are to be like: 'He also predestined [us] to be conformed to the image of His Son' (Rom. 8:29). The ministry of the Holy Spirit towards us is to make us like Christ both in terms of His character and His works (Eph. 2:10). Our goal must be to learn and become who we are in Christ. The apostle Paul writes about this to first-century Christians at Ephesus and reminds them that they have 'learned Christ'; they have 'heard Him'; and they have 'been taught by Him' (Eph. 4:20–23).

Effective Christians have learned the truth as it is in Jesus and it is from this understanding of who we are in Christ and our acceptance of these facts that our behaviour and 'performance' flows. The effectiveness model is not solely based on competence, i.e. successful accomplishment; it is also based on character. The character is the character of Christ – we behave like Him. The competence involved is the competence of Christ – we act like Him and do His work.

There is nothing alien in the idea that how we think about things makes a lot of difference to us. If I change the way I think does that affect the way my life goes? The answer is 'not entirely, but greatly'. In the Christian tradition there are several ways of reflecting on things that enable us to think about them differently. For example, one of the effects of prayer is that it can lead us to think about the events of our lives in a different way.

Understanding yourself and how you think can help you in at least two ways: you can learn how to manage your responses to current events and you can learn how to experience healing from the damage of your past. Understanding that your thoughts are usually a product of your beliefs gives you a tool for exposing those beliefs and dealing with them.

Paul's concept of putting on the mind of Christ and having the mind of Christ, alluded to in an earlier chapter, is hinting at us adopting a different cognitive style.

There is a simple exercise at the close of this chapter that will allow you to relate the Word of God to the specific changes you desire to bring about in your life. Essentially you must do two things with the Scriptures: first you must *personalise* them and second you must *internalise* them.

Personalising the Word of God

A simple example of how to do this would be to take the best-known text of Scripture, John 3:16, which reads:

> *For God so loved the world that He gave His only begotten Son, that whosoever believes in Him should not perish but have everlasting life.*

In place of the words *world* and *whosoever* put your own name. Now read it aloud. Personalising a statement makes it relevant, meaningful and powerful in its effect. When that statement is the Word of God it is also life giving as well as life changing.

I recall as a boy attending a church near us. One of the leaders ran a Bible class for young people and he was an excellent mentor. He had a young family and his son, Arthur, was a friend of mine. One day Arthur showed me a Bible which his parents had given him as a birthday present. It had pictures in it depicting Bible scenes and one of these was an artist's impression of the crucifixion of Christ. Above the picture Arthur's father had written, 'God loves Arthur'. I gazed at the picture and read the words; it was very personal – to Arthur but not to me. I went home and found a Bible similar to Arthur's, with pictures in it. There was one of the crucifixion and I took a pen (sometimes when you have no mentor you have to be a mentor to yourself) and I wrote these words: 'God loves Jim'. As I read the words I looked at the picture and I felt a great wave of emotion sweep over me and, as a little boy, I cried.

I have since discovered something very important about these statements that you make to yourself, which is that when the words you speak are accompanied by an image that is relevant and when this, in turn, carries strong feelings of emotion, then the impact upon you is enormously powerful.

There are two things that make these faith-based statements of fact powerful and effective for you. The first is when you believe them.

When does the Word of God become a life-giving truth?

Suppose you personalise this question and ask it like this: 'At what point does the Word of God become a life-giving truth for me?' The answer is, *the moment you believe it*. Until then it's just words. For example, you may say, 'I believe Christ died.' That is stating an historical fact and you can do it in a detached way. You may go further and say, 'I believe Christ died for mankind.' That is stating a theological fact and you can also do that in a detached way. But if you say, 'I believe Christ died *for me*', you are now stating a personal fact and as you do you will be drawn inexorably towards the truth of it and it will bring you salvation.

The language we speak is important. It is not necessarily the language of reason or logic or even common sense. It is primarily the language of faith. When you personalise the Word of God in this way you are making a very powerful statement about yourself but, more than this, you are making a statement about something that you believe in your heart is true of you.

This is what gives it its power: it is the fact that you believe it.

We only practise what we believe. You might say that you believe something and you can say it as often as you wish and as loudly as you like and as eloquently as you can but if, at the end of it all, you don't actually do it then that means only one thing: *you don't really believe it.* Once you have a belief in your mind you *will* act it out; you can do no other. Beliefs you hold in your mind will be discharged as behaviour, eventually.

The Vocabulary of Faith

A second thing that makes these faith-based statements powerful in their effect upon you is *the way they are worded*. Words on their own do not create a belief but the words cannot be discounted because it is these that express what you feel and believe in your heart to be true. They also serve to impress that belief more deeply upon you by helping you to see yourself in the new situation and to feel the energy of it. Therefore the words you use are important.

As we noted earlier, the Word of God, inspired and applied to us by the Spirit of God, is the primary means of replacing our old destructive habits and ways with new, life-giving ones, and this is key to our total transformation. We are to 'lay aside all filthiness and overflow of wickedness, and receive with meekness the implanted Word, which is able to save your souls' (Jas. 1:21).

This is the source from which the new, life-giving 'scripts' are created and crafted. It's good to put them down in written form. This forces you to use words and this is an important discipline because if you can't put your thoughts into actual words it usually means either you don't understand it well enough or you're not thinking about it clearly enough.

Keep them *personal*, it's about you, and it shows you own the statement. Mix the Word with faith and believe that what it is saying is describing you.

Put them in the *present tense*. Write, speak and think about the desired change, whether habit, attitude, behaviour or objective as though it had *already taken place*.

Bring them to life by using words that work for you; not just a set of quietly reassuring words or words that you understand, but let them be the kind that inspire you and fill you with emotion.

There is great wisdom in these prophetic words from the Old Testament:

Write the vision and make it plain on tablets, that he may run who reads it. (Hab. 2:2)

Write it down in words that make the meaning clear to you and which inspire you to act. Then begin declaring it to yourself as the truth about you, based upon the word of God. Here is an example:

> *Then the word of the LORD came to me, saying: 'Before I formed you in the womb I knew you; before you were born I sanctified you; I ordained you a prophet to the nations.' Then said I: 'Ah, Lord GOD! Behold, I cannot speak for I am a youth.' But the LORD said to me: 'Do not say, "I am a youth," for you shall go to all to whom I send you, and whatever I command you, you shall speak. Do not be afraid of their faces, for I am with you to deliver you.'* (Jer. 1:4–8)

Notice the words 'do not say', that is, 'don't listen to your own voice; listen to My voice'. What might Jeremiah have said to himself? Here is a suggestion:

> *'I am called by God to do this work. I go boldly, courageously, enthusiastically to whoever God sends me and I speak the words He gives me to say to them and He is always there to help me and support me.'*

Certainly something like this would be going through his mind; these words or others like them would be the ones that expressed his belief about himself in this context.

Internalising the Word

This is the second thing you must do. Take the Word of God and make it a part of you so that it is essential to the way you function as a person. 'Your Words were found and I ate them,' says the prophet Jeremiah (Jer. 15:16). Eating the Words of God means internalising them and allowing their meaning to become a reality in your life.

You can do this by continually meditating on the Word you have found (this is discussed in more detail in the following chapter). Another way to internalise the word is to keep repeating it to yourself until these statements that you have crafted become part of your inner dialogue. The word does not have to possess you in the sense that you fully understand what it means, it only has to permeate the unconscious to become part of you and thereby do its work.

H.W.T.L.W.

Dawson Trottman, founder of the Christian organisation known as The Navigators had a piece of advice he liked to share with others as well as follow himself: 'His Word the last word.'[38] By that he meant letting the last words you dwelt upon before dropping off to sleep be the words of the living God. The promise contained in the book of Proverbs speaks volumes in this respect:

When you sleep, they will keep you; and when you awake, they will speak with you. For the commandment is a lamp, and the law a light. (Prov. 6:22–23)

When the Holy Spirit is forming the ways of God in you through the Word of God and new beliefs, habits and attitudes are beginning to build, you will find at times that your actual behaviour and actions don't match the way you are beginning to see yourself in your mind as the new man in Christ. If you observe this happening and sense that it's because you are listening to the wrong message or acting out the wrong script, then you must change it. Here's how you can do this:

Recognise that the next situation brings the opportunity to respond correctly and calls for conscious action not uncontrolled reaction.

Say 'Stop!' Say it out loud if necessary. Before reacting to the situation as you normally would, pause and in a conscious, deliberate way tell yourself, 'This is not me, I'm not like this.' Recognise that the next situation will bring you an opportunity to respond correctly. Remind yourself of the proper script; repeat the words to yourself and resolve that this is how you will act the next time the same situation arises.

Restoring the Lost Image

There are broadly three things that human beings seek instinctively for their lives: security, self-worth and significance. The early chapters of the Bible describe the scenario in which the 'Fall of Man' took place and show how the progenitors of the human race lost these three things. They have been replaced by fear, worry, anxiety, feelings of unworthiness, guilt and shame, giving rise to many 'complexes'. The word 'complex' is often glibly, but not always accurately, used. A complex is a group of emotionally charged ideas ranged around one central idea, rather like the fingers and thumb of a hand held together by the palm.

It's important to distinguish a *complex* from a *repressed complex*. A repressed complex is a system of emotionally charged ideas which get pushed down into the unconscious part of the mind because its presence in the conscious mind is distasteful to the personality, but which carries on functioning in the unconscious, as we have seen, producing all kinds of morbid outcomes.

All complexes are not like this. They do not lead to irrational, inexplicable behaviour. In fact, every mind is full of complexes which will modify behaviour and actions, so that these have little to do with the person's ability and everything to do with their beliefs. There is one complex that is well known. It is talked about and even joked about more than any of the others and it deserves attention here because of its relation to the renewing of the mind.

The inferiority complex

An inferiority complex is a group of ideas, the central one of which is 'I can't'. It stems from a disbelief in yourself and in your value to the community of which you are part, and in your abilities to accomplish or cause things to happen. Integral to this is a strong feeling of helplessness and fear which tends to drive you away from certain situations. It may make you dislike going into the company of others or fearful of meeting strangers or of being in unfamiliar places. It causes you to shrink from anything difficult or that may attract criticism.

You may ask why an inferiority complex concerns us when so many others do not. Why is it spoken about so much? The primary reason is because it militates against self-realisation and frustrates our quest for security, self-worth and significance. It produces many compensatory behaviours which are unwholesome and negative.

We should recognise and accept that self-realisation, which is the harmonious functioning of every possibility within us, is a legitimate and good thing to seek. It depends on believing in ourselves as personalities whom God has entrusted with certain gifts and who have a contribution to make to society and the Kingdom of God that no one else can make.

Because we have a wish for the power to 'be' and 'do' we also have two forces in our mind going in opposite directions. One is saying 'I can', the other is saying 'I can't'. If someone has an inferiority complex, then 'I can't' is much stronger than 'I can'.

The renewing of the mind calls for a weakening of 'I can't' and a strengthening of 'I can'.

All of us sit somewhere on the continuum that stretches between 'I can't' and 'I can'. This reflects the belief we have about our ability to cause something to happen. It has been remarked already that most of the goals we set are not based upon our ability to achieve them but upon the beliefs we hold about ourselves and, for the Christian, it is the source and justification for this belief that matters.

High achievers, effective people, without exception, all sit close to the 'I can' end of the scale and they attempt big things. People at the other end of the scale avoid the challenge.

It's useless telling someone who has a low level of belief in their ability to cause things to happen to 'think big' or 'dream large' because they are 'programmed', if you will, by their own self-perception to think small or not dream at all. Test this out on yourself: what kind of goals do you have? Are they big or modest? Do they reflect wishful thinking or do you really believe you're going to see them realised?

What if your belief in your ability to cause things to happen is low, can it be changed? The answer is 'yes' and we can learn how from an Old Testament 'high achiever' whose name was David. He became a king but at the time under consideration he was just a humble shepherd.

His brothers were soldiers in an army that was joined in battle with the army of the Philistines. When he went to visit them, he witnessed something; a giant warrior named Goliath stepped out from the ranks of the Philistines and challenged the men of Israel to nominate themselves a champion who would fight single handed with him to decide the outcome of the battle and the future of their respective peoples.

The Old Testament records the response to this: 'All the men of Israel, when they saw the man, fled from him and were dreadfully afraid' (1 Sam. 17:24).

Our personal 'I can' quotient is linked to our self-perception; belief drives behaviour, every time!

David's response is quite different: 'Let no man's heart fail because of him . . . [I] will go and fight with this Philistine' (1 Sam. 17:31).

These are not empty words spoken by a foolish youth. David's belief in his causative power was high, for very good reasons. His perception of the kind of person he believed himself to be was quite different from the others who ran away. His perception of the situation was different because his inner dialogue was different. What was about to unfold was not based upon bravado or positive thinking; it came about because of something far greater than any of these.

David's words to King Saul revealed what it was.

> *'Your servant used to keep his father's sheep, and when a lion or a bear came and took a lamb out of the flock, I went after it and struck it, and delivered the lamb from its mouth . . . Your servant has killed both lion and bear . . . The LORD, who delivered me from the paw of the lion and . . . the bear, He will deliver me from the hand of this Philistine.'* (1 Sam. 17:34–37)

The first way in which this power of 'I can' is developed is through *personal mastery*. We know, through past experience, that when through faith in God we applied ourselves we succeeded and progressed. We have encountered similar situations before and we can do it again. Success builds on success.

David went to meet the giant Philistine and cried,

> *'I come to you in the name of the LORD of hosts, the God of the armies of Israel . . . This day the LORD will deliver you into my hand, and I will strike you and take your head from you.'* (1 Sam. 17:45–46)

A second way in which 'I can' is developed is through *vicarious experiences*. By watching others and their efforts we become aware that we can do similar things.

Since we are surrounded by so great a cloud of witnesses, let us . . . [do as they did] . . . run with endurance the race that is set before us. (Heb. 12:1)

These are the heroes of faith described in an earlier chapter. They are not spectators watching us but we are to look at them and learn that what God did for them and through them He can do for us as well.

A third way to develop this 'can do' attitude is through *social persuasion*. We are enabled by another's belief in us and encouragement of us, to build the belief in our capability that 'through Christ we can'.

David had no social persuasion to help him on this occasion. Instead he had to battle with social dissuasion! This underscores the need for us to be careful who we listen to. If David had listened to his brothers or even to King Saul himself, he would never have gone to fight Goliath.

There are those whose counsel is to discourage us from trying. You'll hear suggestions like:

'You haven't got what it takes.'

'You lack the intelligence, you haven't had the education you need.'

'People from your background never succeed at this.'

If you listen to this and accept it, it becomes a part of you; your behaviour follows, your expectations get lower and, guess what, you'll start finding evidence everywhere you look that this is the 'truth' about you.

But where social persuasion is in the form of encouragement and it serves your God-given purpose then accept it! Make it personal, speak it to yourself. Let it become the language of faith for you.

A splendid example of this is given through these words written by the apostle Paul who said, 'I can do all things through Christ who strengthens me' (Phil. 4:13).

This is the language (inner dialogue) of someone who knows who he is and who is clear about the work he has to do. These words do more than hint at the kind of person he believed himself to be and the belief he had in his ability to cause things to happen. They spell out the source and the secret of it.

The missionary journeys of the apostle Paul are legendary. He travelled three times around the then known world; no mean feat in those days. He promoted Christ and the Christian way and communicated the gospel of Christ effectively wherever he went. In doing this he crossed not only geographical boundaries but cultural ones as well, which is a much harder thing to do.

He planted churches and established the Christian faith. He wrote more than half the New Testament and his influence continues to this day since much of our theology comes from what he wrote under the inspiration of God's Spirit. The meaning and significance of these three things – what you are telling yourself; how you are seeing yourself and what you believe you can accomplish – are writ large across this man's life and if we would see the godly transformation we seek in our own lives, we must follow his example

In the next chapter we'll look in detail about how this works in practice but, before you turn to that, why not pause and use some of the questions and suggestions that follow to help you engage with the concepts discussed in this chapter?

Pause and be aware of your internal dialogue. Make a note of the things you say to yourself and of what triggers them. Use the examples below to help.

Statements I Make to Myself

(These are the things you believe about yourself in a given situation.)

- *It's no use, I'll never succeed*
- *I am inferior*
- *God doesn't love me*
- *People don't like me*
- *My childhood will always affect me*
- *I deserve to be punished for my mistakes*
- *If people cared for me they'd know what I want*
- *I can't change the way I think*
- *People are not to be trusted*
- *People should trust me*
- *I must never tell people what I think*
- *I'll never be any good*
- *I can't do anything right*
- *I must never show weakness*
- *I must never get upset*

What 'Triggers' These Statements?

(These are the feelings you may have while you are in the situation.)

- *When I feel no one cares about me*
- *When I feel tense*
- *When I feel depressed*
- *When I feel afraid*
- *When I feel happy with everything*
- *When I'm full of resentments*
- *When I feel belittled*
- *When I can't control a situation*
- *When my self-worth is being attacked*
- *When I feel fed up with life*
- *When there are rows and arguments at home*
- *When I feel I'm being punished unjustly*
- *When I feel disappointed about being let down*
- *When there are problems at work*
- *When I feel tired*

What have you learned from this? You may see a pattern develop where perhaps two or three of the above apply to you more than the others.

Select two or three of the above statements that often apply to you.

Now consider the following biblical facts about you (below) and decide which of them would help you dispute the belief statements you commonly make about yourself.

- *I am secure and safe*
- *I am precious to God*
- *I am worthwhile to God*
- *I am significant and important to God*
- *I am loveable to God*
- *I am not guilty before God*
- *I am competent and capable of obeying and pleasing God*
- *I can do everything God wants me to do*
- *God is in control, nothing can happen to me without His permission*
- *Nothing is ever 'awful' or 'terrible' for me now*
- *I don't have to understand everything that is going on for me to trust God with my security, self-worth and significance*

Pull the outcomes of the above together – your beliefs, your feelings and the biblical facts – and create a script that affirms the truth for you.

Thank God for the truth – repeatedly and out loud.

Affirm it as a statement of fact.

CHAPTER FIVE
Effective Lives
The Paths to Power

There can be no success without preparation and there can be no preparation without discipline. (Anon.)

Your name shall no longer be called Jacob, but Israel; for you have struggled with God and with men, and have prevailed. (Gen. 32:28)

These who have turned the world upside down are come here also. (Acts 17:6)

Effective Christians are men and women of faith, prayer and the Word who also possess the kind of mindset that enables them to cooperate with the Divine purpose and plan.

In this chapter we are going to explore how the principles and concepts of the book are applied through the practice of four major disciplines as the means of empowering our lives and making them effective.

The first part of this book has been focused upon *knowing ourselves*. That is, about understanding how we function as human beings and also as spiritual beings who relate to God through faith in Jesus Christ.

This next part concentrates on *knowing God* and will deal with four areas of Christian thought and practice to which you should now begin to apply yourself. These are key drivers in the Christian's life and will expand it in terms of its spiritual power and effectiveness.

As we noted in an earlier chapter when discussing the three enabling factors of faith, prayer and the Word of God, these four areas of application are not meant to be performed solely as matters of religious duty or perceived as doctrines to be stored in your mind as so much information. They are to be fashioned into your life to such an extent that they become an integral part of your makeup and function for you as naturally as eating or sleeping or breathing. Together they create the context in which the thought patterns and habits that make for effectiveness can develop and truly work.

Hallmarks of Effectiveness

If you will apply yourself in these areas then there are four major outcomes which you can expect in your life as a result and these are:

1. *Success* which is the result of meditating upon the word of God.[39]
2. *Power* which comes as a result of engaging in prayer.[40]
3. *Relevance* which is the consequence of being guided by God and connected to His purposes.[41]
4. *Usefulness* which springs from adopting the mantle of service.[42]

Success: the truest definition of success came from Christ Himself when He said to His disciples, 'My food is to do the will of

Him who sent Me and to finish His work' (John 4:34). This has profound implications for every follower of Christ. Think of all the lepers He did not heal, all the miracles He did not perform, all the places He never visited; Christ left everything undone except His Father's will and for us to be able to claim at the end of our life, as He did at the end of His, 'I have finished the work which You have given Me to do' (John 17:4) is success *par excellence.*

This success comes to those whose minds and hearts are possessed by the Word of God. They have knowledge, direction and motivation as a consequence and they act in accordance with it to successfully advance the Kingdom of God, not their own interests.

Power through prayer: Prayer is a force that can move the heavenly world and bring its power down to earth. That this faculty should be in the hands of ordinary men is remarkable. The insightful words of C.S. Lewis pinpoint the key issue here:

The prayer preceding all prayers is, 'May it be the real I who speaks. May it be the real Thou that I speak to.'[43]

This is our challenge.

Relevance is a much needed feature of the Christian's contribution in today's society. We are cast into the midst of life to be salt and light in the communities of which we are part. Paul's great cry is for Christians to be 'filled with the knowledge of His [God's] will' (Col. 1:9). Only as we are guided in accordance with the Divine will can we be relevant to the needs of the hour by being in the right place, doing the right things and with a proper sense of timing.

True *usefulness* is an asset that is impossible to overestimate and it is the key to greatness. The words of Christ to His disciples and also about Himself confirm these things. 'I am among you as the One who serves' (Luke 22:27) denotes the spirit of service linked to a great purpose and this leads to usefulness of the highest order imaginable.

These four – success, power, relevance and usefulness – are hallmarks of the effective life and come from knowing God in the deep spiritual sense of that word and from following His way. They are not to be seen or pursued as ends in themselves but as the means through which a far greater end is fulfilled.

The four short case histories that follow will help us see more closely how this works in practice, together with the outcomes that flow from it.

Case Study One
Joshua and the Practice of Meditation
(Josh. 1:1–8; Ps. 1:1–3)

This Book of the Law shall not depart from your mouth, but you shall meditate in it day and night, that you may observe to do according to all that is written in it. For then you will make your way prosperous, and then you will have good success. (Josh. 1:8)

Joshua (1485–1375 BC)

His name means 'the Lord is salvation'. He was head of the tribe of Ephraim. He was reared in slavery in Egypt and, following the Exodus, he became a soldier, military leader and was a personal aide of Moses.

He was one of the twelve spies whom Moses sent to investigate the Promised Land (Num. 13). The report which he and another leader, Caleb, brought back was positive and encouraging and in sharp contrast to the gloomy, depressing report of the other ten spies.

He was Moses' assistant and at the age of eighty succeeded Moses as national leader. He led the people into the Promised Land and oversaw its conquest.

He exhorted Israel to obey God's Law (Josh. 23). He was called the servant of the Lord (Josh. 24:29) and died at the age of one hundred and ten.

As a man, Joshua was habitually 'in the Word'. This implies that the 'Word' was in him. He was not merely familiar with it as an expert might be, able to explain it, extol its virtues and argue from it where necessary, but by implication the Word of God was woven into his psyche; it was an integral part of his makeup. It influenced his thinking, informed his speech, motivated his actions and guided his behaviour. This practice and the results it produced accounted for his success as a military leader, national statesman, family man and great human being.

The process of meditation, which leads to this condition of soul and spirit, is more than reading or reciting the Word of God. It implies personalising it and internalising it, as we discussed in the previous chapter, to the extent that it becomes a part of you. A synonym for 'meditate' is the word 'ruminate'. This means chewing something with the teeth to make it fit for the stomach.

The words of the prophet Jeremiah suggest this: 'Your Words were found and I ate them, and your Word was to me the joy and rejoicing of my heart' (Jer. 15:16). This means making it personal so that it's about you, no one else. It also means taking the words and believing they are describing something that is true of you, or true for you now, even though it may not yet be.

It means you see yourself being, doing and having what the Word is saying to you and seeing this in a way that is clear, vivid and powerful. The more you can see yourself being like this and behaving like this, the stronger the impact will be upon you.

You must also feel the emotional impact of the words. The Old Testament prophets described the emotion they felt as they experienced themselves in the situation envisaged by the Word that came to them: 'joy and rejoicing' (Jer. 15:16); 'it was in my mouth like honey in sweetness' (Ezek. 3:3). Christ in the New

Testament said, 'My food is to do the will of Him that sent Me, and to finish His work' (John 4:34). In other words, 'this is what refreshes and invigorates me'.

You do this with God's Word. Keep telling its truth to yourself. Meditate means literally re-speaking the Word: to ponder by talking to yourself.

How Do You Meditate?

The process of meditation is one of active recitation, literally a re-speaking of God's words as self-talk, so that they form the basis of the conversation you are having with yourself. Experientially you are 'in' what is being described; you see yourself being, doing and having the thing you are talking to yourself about and feel the joyous emotion of actually doing this.

The purpose of meditation is 'that you may observe to do all that it says' (see Josh. 1:8). Meditation means much more than just contemplation or study. It implies reflecting upon God's Word in a thoughtful way that causes you to appropriate what it says personally and apply it to your life. This is mixing the Word with faith to generate belief and action (Heb. 4:2).

Far from emptying your mind and then waiting for something to enter it, meditation is a matter of consciously filling your mind with God's Word and allowing that same Word to generate thoughts within your mind that instruct and inform and inspire and direct you. Scripture comes to us as text, enabling us to learn what God reveals. But as we ponder the words of Scripture we realise that it comes not simply to inform us but to form us in the sense of making us participants in the action it proposes and enabling us to live and follow in the way of Christ.

C.S. Lewis was a man who made a daily effort to live in God's presence through being 'in the Word'. He said,

> *The real problem of the Christian life comes . . . the very moment you wake up each morning. All your wishes and hopes for the day rush at you like wild animals. And the first job each morning consists simply in shoving them all back; in listening to that other voice, taking that other point of view, letting that other larger, stronger, quieter life come flowing in. And so on, all day.*[44]

Meditation is 'desiring and hearing the voice of the living God' and Joshua's secret lay in the fact that he was that kind of person. He was a man who was habitually 'in the Word'.

More than Positive Thinking

If you trust in 'the law of the mind' you will get what the law of the mind gives. But if you trust in the Law of the Lord, you'll get what it gives.

> *Meditate in it, day and night . . . do according to all that is written . . . then you will make your way prosperous and . . . have good success.* (Josh. 1.8)

Meditating in the day implies a conscious activity. Meditating in the night implies a subconscious activity. The words of Moses to the people of Israel describe the entire process (Deut. 6:1–9). First, the Word is *absorbed* and becomes active within us by speaking it to ourselves as something we believe. Second, it is *reinforced* through heartfelt conversations we have with others, through teaching it to others and by using even mechanical means to keep it in the forefront of our vision.

The wise words found in the book of Proverbs hint at the subconscious payback that comes through meditating on the Word (Prov. 6:21–23).

Set aside time each day to meditate on the Word of God. You can find the Word to meditate upon in at least three ways.

First, through due diligence (daily reading of the Word). Then, if or when something you read gives you pause for thought, stop and ponder it.

This may lead you into a second, different phase where you find yourself dallying with the words instead of wolfing them down as information. Be prepared for this and be willing to spend the time doing it.

Third, through your circumstances. Instead of finding the Word, the Word 'finds' you! Your circumstances are not the Word but they call it to mind and you can begin a dialogue with it that is revealing and profitable (1 Kgs 19:8–18).

Reflection

Pause and reflect on this:

A Meditation: Zacchaeus (Luke 19:1–10)

He had to climb a tree because he wanted a better view of Jesus. His view of Him had been obscured by the crowd but in his heart this was not satisfactory. So at some cost and personal difficulty he removed himself to a vantage point from which he could see Him.

However, his presence was neither accident nor surprise to Jesus. He came by and He knew of his presence and his name. He called Zacchaeus by his name – come down!

You must now come down the tree and invite Jesus into your house; into your church. The effect of this will be radical transformation of many things people have assumed about you and that you have become used to over a number of years.

Here are some questions to start personal reflection:

- What is the 'tree' you have climbed?
- Why have you done it – what are you 'up to'?
- Is there anything in your life at present that is causing you to stop and ponder?
- In what ways do you think God may be trying to get your attention?
- Is there a word of Scripture that you feel you ought to begin to meditate upon?
- What have you learned from this meditation?

Case Study Two
Daniel: Power Through Prayer

Prayer is the power by which that comes to pass which would not otherwise take place. (Andrew Murray)[45]

He prayed . . . as was his custom since early days. (Dan. 6:10)

Daniel (6th century BC)

A Jewish exile who had been deported to Babylon during the reign of King Nebuchadnezzar. As a well-educated Jew he was selected for special training in the palace in Babylon and rose to become a high-ranking civil servant serving in three successive administrations.

He was thrown into a den of lions and survived the experience as a result of a miraculous deliverance.

He was the author of a number of significant prophecies.

It was said that 'an excellent spirit was in him'; the testimony of those who knew him confirmed that the roots of this excellence were traceable back to his relationship with God (Dan. 5:11–14).

He was a man of extraordinary faith and belief in God who maintained the integrity of his beliefs in a visible way, while serving without compromise as a high-profile public figure in a society that was anti-God.

Like Joshua before him, he was effective. His life and ministry influenced his own generation and succeeding generations, right up to the present day. He lived in the midst of momentous events and while the direct impact he had on the community of exiles in

Babylon cannot be known, he was a force for good as far as the Babylonians themselves were concerned.

Promises Become Prayers

Daniel's prayers are compelling. They are founded upon a study of Scripture and they grow out of an understanding of the nature of the times in which he lived and of the needs those times represent. The Word of God becomes the dialect of prayer. Daniel is not divorced from the reality of what is taking place or of what will yet take place. His prayers are personal and he prays as someone who, despite his position, is affected and touched by events as they unfold and the promises in God's Word become not only the foundation for his prayer but the vehicle for expressing it. They reflect his unfaltering belief in a God who reveals His Word to those who ask, and responds to those who pray according to that Word (Dan. 9:2–19).

Prayer based on the Word of God is also the method of holy argument for Daniel. Abraham found this as he prayed (Gen. 18:23–33). Christ responded to it in the case of the Gentile woman who came to Him (Matt. 15:22–28). And Christ Himself used this method of holy argument through prayer in His Sermon on the Mount (Matt. 7:7–11).

Prayers Become Prophecies

Notice the progression in this activity. Prayers that are affirmations of Divine facts carry assurances of Divine blessings (Jas. 5:15). Christ taught His followers about this predictive element in prayer:

So Jesus answered and said to them, 'Have faith in God. For assuredly, I say to you, whoever says to this mountain, "Be removed and be cast into the sea," and does not doubt in his heart, but believes that those things he says will be done, he will have whatever he says. Therefore I say to you, whatever things you ask when you pray, believe that you receive them, and you shall have them.' (Mark 11:22–24)

Prayer is a force that can move the heavenly world and bring its power down to earth and we have positive assurance from God that if we will call on Him, He will answer us in ways that will astound us (Jer. 33:3).

Much is made of Daniel's life, and rightly so, but the significance of prayer in his life should not be overlooked or minimised; it is one of the great keys to his effectiveness as a man of God among men. He had 'power with God and with men' (Gen. 32:28 AMP) largely as a consequence of persisting and ultimately prevailing, in prayer (Dan. 9:20–23).

There are two important aspects to the prayers of Daniel that concern us here. The first is that many of his prayers were prayers of *petition* and this is the aspect we have just discussed. The second is that many of his prayers took the form of *confession* (Dan. 9:4–20). Petition is well known and understood: confession, perhaps less so.

Confession takes place when we acknowledge a fault or wrongdoing as ours and we admit it to God, to our self and sometimes others using words that describe the fault accurately and that express what we feel about it. This, in some ways, is the opposite of petition.

Petition requires us to ask in faith using words that describe what we want, and which help us to envision the reality of it as though it were already ours and also to express and feel the emotion associated with possessing it.

In the previous chapter we discussed the creation and use of 'faith statements', sometimes called 'affirmations' or 'scripts'. These are based upon the Word of God (that's important) which may come to us in the form of commands to obey, wisdom to act upon, promises to claim and, in that sense, they are really confessions of *faith*.

But there is another side to this coin, if you will, and it is revealed as we consider the need to confess our *faults*. Like the other, this also involves the use of words and they have to be of the kind that personalise the fault, like 'I' and 'my' and 'mine' and which pinpoint it in ways that specify it precisely, cause us to visualise it clearly and feel the emotion of it.

Why do it?

A study of Daniel's prayers show that confession is made to 'get rid of the rubbish' and remove the things that would hurt, harm and hinder us and our relationship with God.

Confession and Repression

In psychological terms there are basically five ways in which the feelings we have get discharged as behaviour. Briefly stated, these are:

- *legitimate physical means*, i.e. biological expression.
- *sublimation*, redirecting the energies into some other channel that serves the community and satisfies the soul.

- *perversion* is where the behavioural instincts are not let out in the right way. A person finds there is nothing he or she can do or be and so, in their impatience to express themselves, they engage in behaviour that is anti-social or abnormal.
- *suppression* or *self-control* is conscious, voluntary control of behaviours that cannot or ought not to be expressed.
- *repression* was briefly referred to in chapter three. Repression occurs when an event or experience that is distasteful or abhorrent to our personality, for example a traumatic fear, worry, shock or sin, is deliberately but unwittingly pushed down into the depths of the unconscious mind. However, the *feelings* associated with the event or events, whatever they may be, can manifest themselves as *behaviours* that are seemingly unrelated to their cause and are often unwholesome and damaging to the individual. King David, after his sin with Bathsheba, described the effects of his repressed feelings: 'When I kept silent, my bones grew old . . . For day and night Your hand was heavy upon me; my vitality was turned into the drought of summer' (Ps. 32:2–4).

Confession is the key that brings the release which we need. It is not just a psychological exercise which has a therapeutic value. Confession has a spiritual dimension. True confession is the result of repentance and is linked to redemption and forgiveness and brings healing and wholeness to our inner being (Ps. 32:5; Prov. 28:13).

Confession is the primary means of dealing with the unwholesome effects of repression and the Scriptures allow us to broaden the concept to include confession to ourselves and others. 'Confess your sins to each other and pray for each other so that you may be healed' (Jas. 5:16 NLT).

The words of *The Book of Common Prayer* (AD 1549) amplify this in a helpful way:

> *If there be any of you who cannot quiet his own conscience herein but require further comfort or counsel, let him come to some other minister of the word of God and open his grief.*

When we confess in the presence of another, using words that pinpoint the failure or the fear or the anxiety that plagues us and which personalise the issue in a way that makes us accountable for it, then the confession becomes very real and powerful in its effect. As long as we are by ourselves in the confession of our faults and failings everything remains in the dark, but when this is done in the presence of a trusted confidante, everything is brought into the light.

Before you decide to dismiss this as impractical and unworkable, test the validity of it simply by trying it and you'll discover the cleansing and healing power it brings. Dietrich Bonhoeffer, the German pastor, theologian and a key founding member of the Confessing Church movement said:

> *Confession is the God-given remedy for self-deception and self-indulgence. When we confess our sins before a brother Christian, we are mortifying the pride of the flesh and delivering it up to shame and death through Christ.*[46]

How to Make Prayer Effective

The most frequently used word for prayer in the Bible is *proseuchamai*. It means 'an invocation, request or entreaty in the direction of God'. Prayer has to be directed (Ps. 5:3). This makes it a definite activity. It is never a vague calling out into an empty void to test whether there is anyone there. 'He who comes to God must believe that He is and that He is a rewarder of those who diligently seek Him' (Heb. 11:6).

Christ's teaching on prayer emphasised that it is to be directed to God, the Father (Matt. 6:6). This directed nature of prayer leads us to think of three practical things.

1. Prayer must be focused

What does this mean and how might we do it? Jesus, in His Sermon on the Mount, emphasised the need to be *specific* (Matt. 6:6). We should have a specific *time* set aside for prayer – 'when you pray'. If you don't make time for this you will never find time! Daniel prayed three times a day (Dan. 6:10). The frequency of his praying suggests planned prayer times requiring time and specific timing. This doesn't exclude spontaneous prayer which can take place anytime and may be triggered when facing a crisis, making an important decision or when you're faced with a problem.

Something else that helps the focus is when we identify a specific *place* where we can pray. Daniel had his upper room; Christ said 'enter your closet'. This infers a specific place to which we go when we pray; a place where we can avoid distraction. Christ often went out into a lonely or solitary place when He wanted to pray. Can you think of a place like this that could become a place of prayer for you?

A third thing that helps create a focus is to *perform a ritual*, however simple. Daniel opened his window towards Jerusalem and knelt down on his knees and prayed. Christ said 'shut the door'. These things may seem as nothing but they facilitate a steady, deliberate, premeditated act.

2. Prayer must be intentional

What is the purpose of your prayer? Here are a few suggestions, from Daniel's example.

First, *communion with God*. Beyond conversation which is communication, there is communion which is about fellowship and togetherness. Prayer is more than getting answers.

Next, *giving to God*, for example giving thanks or praise or making confession. Again the intention of prayer can be to *receive from God* – guidance, strength, revelation. Prayer is more than talking; it also includes listening (1 Chron. 29:18; Hab. 2:2).

Finally, *cooperating with God*. Being in an attitude of prayer helps create conditions that are conducive to hearing God's voice, discerning God's will and committing ourselves to Him by faith. Be clear about your intentions when you come to pray.

3. Directed prayer is relational

It is not a psychological exercise that tunes the senses and satisfies the intellect and helps our emotional well-being. It is a devotional experience. When we pray we are relating directly with God Himself and the potential outcomes are awesome.

Becoming Effective through Prayer

'This kind does not go out but by prayer and fasting' (Matt. 17:21). Christ spoke these words to His disciples after they had failed in their efforts to bring a cure for the child who was ill.

Fasting produces an intensity of spirit when praying; it creates a strong sense of focus, is a powerful aid to spiritual concentration and is seen in Scripture as promoting effective prayer.

Fasting is not a 'hunger strike'; it is literally 'doing without while doing within'. There are three types of fast detailed in the Scriptures:

- *The normal fast*: this is where you go without food but not without water e.g. Temptation of Christ (Matt. 4:2).
- *The absolute fast*: this is where you go without food or water e.g. Paul at the time of his conversion (Acts 9:9) and also during a time of national crisis (Esther 4:16).
- *The partial fast*: this is where you keep to a simple, restricted diet (Dan. 10:3).

Christ gave instructions to His disciples about fasting (Matt. 6:16–18) and there are also examples of fasting in the early church (Acts 14:23).

- Why should we fast? Here are some biblical reasons:
- When personal sanctity is being sought. (Ps. 69:10)
- When seeking God in order to prevail with Him. (Ezra 8:23)
- To obtain deliverance (God's chosen fast). (Isa. 58:6)
- For revelation and guidance. (Dan. 9:2–3, 21–22)

Make a Habit of Praying

Three Men in a Boat

There is a story concerning three men who went off fishing in a boat. But the mist came down and visibility got poor and the sea became rough and choppy. The men grew scared and became fearful for their safety so they decided to pray. The spokesman for the three stood up in the boat, doffed his cap and began, 'O Lord, you know we've never bothered you with anything before but if you will just help us to safety we promise you, we'll never bother you with anything again!'

You cannot pray by default, it has to be by design. We learn this from Daniel. To be effective through prayer we must cultivate it until it becomes a habit. Changing is not easy. Your old habits are designed to keep you as you are. You will meet tremendous resistance when you try to change. The secret is to make the new more dominant and more desirable in your mind than the old and, at the same time, continually think and speak of yourself as being in the new way.

It is important that you establish a prayer habit that is appropriate for you – not one that is imposed on you.

The words of Alfred, Lord Tennyson are often quoted and ought to inspire prayer:

Pray for my soul. More things are wrought by prayer Than this world dreams of. Wherefore let thy voice, Rise like a fountain for me night and day.[47]

Reflection

Pause and reflect on the following:

> *If you have faith as a mustard seed, you will say to this mountain [obstacle/impossible situation/problem/thing you want to change], 'Move from here to there,' and it will move.* (Matt. 17:20)[48]

How might this work out in your life in practice? Here's a clue: don't think about what you don't want, think about what you do want. We're drawn towards what we think about, remember?

Think what it would look like if the 'mountain' in your life was gone. Describe how you feel now that the 'mountain' has gone.

Let this become the basis of your prayer. Allow the Word of God to test and inform your thinking and desires then let your prayer be made clearly, specifically and passionately.

Think of two or three people whose lives have inspired and instructed you. Can you use them as a role model?

- What things cause you to pray? Are there any more that should be on your list?
- What areas do you feel you need to work on to make prayer a habit for you?
- Which aspect of Daniel's prayer life inspires you most?
- What might be a prayer project for you?

Case Study Three
Joseph: How Divine Guidance Makes Us Effective and Relevant
(Gen. 37:1–36; 39 – 50:26)

One of the twelve sons of the Old Testament patriarch Jacob. He was his father's favourite son and received from him a coat of many colours that marked him as 'the special one'.

His brothers hated him partly out of jealousy and partly because of the way he boasted about the destiny he would fulfil. They tried to destroy him but failed.

Joseph had a 'dream' (Gen. 37:5) – it did not arise from within his own human psyche but it came from God and foretold a destiny he was to fulfil. His dreams had drawing power and became a driving force in his life. He had his fair share of difficulties, drawbacks and even disasters.[49] But he held to his dream and kept faith with the God who had given it and this led him towards his destiny.[50]

Joseph was a guided man and throughout the events that shaped his life, and made him what he was, he remained relevant and effective.

Effectiveness and Connectedness

A key message from Joseph's life is that our effectiveness depends on our connectedness. We live in a connected universe, 'All things work together for good . . .' (Rom. 8:28). It is not a meaningless, chaotic system full of random associations and events, even though it may seem to be that way at times. The Greek word used here is *teleos* which means 'having an ultimate goal or purpose'. The universe and everything in it is not out of control; it is under control and is being guided towards an ultimate goal.

Likewise, Christians are a connected people, '. . . those who love God, to those who are called according to His purpose' (Rom. 8:28). We have a sense of purpose; we know who we are, why we're here and where we are going. We are 'teleological' in nature and we are being guided towards a goal. 'As many as are led by the spirit of God, these are sons of God' (Rom. 8:14).

How to Become a Connected Person

Here are four important things we can expect and must look for. Connected (guided) people have . . .

1. A strong sense of Purpose[51]

They know why they are here and what their role and function is in life. Allow yourself to reflect on this for a moment and be challenged by it.

2. A strong sense of Place[52]

It is not the place but the intensity of your presence in that place which counts. Are you in the right place? Does it release you or restrict you? Enable you or cripple you?

What matters isn't what's happening to you in that place but the kind of contribution you are able to make.

3. A strong sense of Passion[53]

In relation to your purpose how focused are you? Is it a hobby or calling? What kind of priority does it have in your life? How important is it to you in the ordinary, everyday scheme of things? Do you have some kind of project that acts as a vehicle for its fulfilment? And how far are you willing to take it, what price are you prepared to pay?

4. A strong sense of Presence[54]

Our effectiveness depends upon our connectedness. Think of the 'prospering presence' in Joseph's story; it is the secret of his effectiveness and it made his contribution relevant in all of life's circumstances.

Joseph had an intuitive sense of the presence of God, he was in tune with the Word of God and he was in touch with his circumstances

We are not left to our own devices (Ps. 16:11). God has promised to give us direction according to His will and purpose for us and this comes through the Holy Scriptures,[55] the Holy Spirit,[56] spiritual gifts,[57] circumstances,[58] counsellors[59] and an inward witness.[60]

Reflection

Pause and reflect on this:

How 'connected' do you think you are i.e. how open are you to being guided (Gen. 24:27)? Which of these words describe you best?

- Guided . . . confused . . . disconnected . . . puzzled . . . in touch . . . in tune
- Where in your life do you need guidance now?

Consider this promise of Guidance from God:

The LORD will guide you continually. (Isa. 58:11)

- What are you telling yourself when you read this?
- What would you like to be able to say when you read this?

Write a short script that powerfully states what your ideal is. Begin with: *'I am . . .'*

- Base your words on the Word of Scripture; listen to the voice of the Holy Spirit not your own spirit. Don't let it be something that is based on your past experience, public opinion, common sense or worse, but let the words reflect your faith in the Word God is speaking to you.
- Look at your words, write them and rewrite them until they reflect the truth of God's Word in a way that inspires and uplifts you and fills you with confidence.
- Then, make it part of your ongoing inner dialogue through repetition.

Scripts like these are powerful when they are faith-full and affirmed prayerfully.

Case Study Four
Paul: Usefulness through Service

Paul, a bondservant of Jesus Christ. (Rom. 1:1)

I was not disobedient to the heavenly vision. (Acts 26:19)

Next to the resurrection of Jesus Christ, the most important thing to have happened in Christendom was the conversion of Saul of Tarsus. It is the remarkable story of how the man who opposed Christ and the Christian way became the servant of Christ and the preacher of the Christian gospel. How the persecutor of the church became its biggest supporter. How a narrow-minded religious bigot became a man with such a breadth of vision that it led him to become a preacher of the gospel to the Gentiles.

He described himself as 'a bondservant of Jesus Christ' and declared that he was 'the least of the apostles, who am not worthy to be called an apostle' (1 Cor. 15:9). He was not a man who suffered from low self-esteem; quite the contrary, he was strong in his ministry and confident in his calling. 'By the grace of God I am what I am, and His grace towards me was not in vain; but I laboured more abundantly than they all, yet not I, but the grace of God which was with me' (1 Cor. 15:10).

Paul chose to be a servant and when we do this we give up the right to be in charge. We become available and vulnerable.

Even though I am a free man with no master, I have become a slave to all people to bring many to Christ. (1 Cor. 9:19 NLT)

This was Paul the apostle and his story shows us that true usefulness lies along the path of service aided by humility. Christ made a revolutionary statement to His followers that sets the standard for all Christian work and the spirit in which it is to be done.

> *You know that the rulers of the Gentiles lord it over them, and their high officials exercise authority over them. Not so with you. Instead, whoever wants to become great among you must be your servant, and whoever wants to be first must be your slave.* (Matt. 20:25–27 NIV)

How Do You See Yourself?

The clue lies in how we see those around us, and how we see others depends to a great extent on how we see ourselves. Look at the list of the following six options and try to decide which best describes you at present. All six are found within family groups, churches, communities, societies and whole nations.

- The Savage: *you are my enemy and I must destroy you*
- The Monarch: *you are my subject and I must subdue you*
- The Master: *you are my servant and I must use you*
- The Benefactor: *you are weak and vulnerable and I must take care of you*
- The Kinsman: *you have equal rights with me and I must treat you with respect*
- The Statesman (servant king): *you have great potential and I will help you realise it*

You may have to study this list for a while before being able to decide where you sit along the continuum between 'savage' and 'servant king'. The life of Christ, the servant King, was geared to giving, not getting. He 'gave' the blind man back his sight. He 'gave' the leper back his health. Whenever Jesus came into a life or a situation he always made things better than they were.

In the world of psychology there is a principle called the Pygmalion principle. Simply stated it says 'people tend to live up to, and act in accordance with, the expectations of others'. Our aim should be to see the best in others and help them become the best they can be.

Effective Christians possess the spirit of service. They cultivate it as a habit and it becomes a way of life. It is one thing to act like a servant but quite another to be a servant. Service is not a list of things we do, though in being a servant we discover things to do.

'I want to' or 'I have to'

Note carefully the 'mindset' of this habit so as not to confuse the servant mind with a servile mind. The servant mind possesses dignity and self-respect. Its motives are love and concern, and the process is voluntary. The key phrase is 'I want to'. The servile mind derives from loss of dignity, low self-esteem and lack of self-worth. Its motive is fear and the process is forced. The key phrase here is 'I have to'. There are very few things in life that any of us *have* to do. In fact some will argue that there is really only one thing we have to do and that is to die. Everything else is a choice.

There is an important clue contained in the phrases 'I choose to' and 'I have to'. Examine your circumstances and notice where you find yourself saying 'I have to do this'. This signals that you're really doing something against your will and if that is so then you can be sure that your unconscious mind will provide you with the creativity and the energy you need to get you out of doing the thing you don't really want to do. In effect, you are working against yourself.

Examine where this is happening then do this: change the 'I have to' into 'I choose to'. This is not simply a matter of semantics; it is an important exercise that will enable you to look at your choices and help you become more authentic. Changing from doing something because you 'have to' to doing it because you 'choose to' may call for a change of attitude.

> *Let this mind be in you which was also in Christ Jesus . . . He made Himself of no reputation, taking the form of a bondservant . . . He humbled Himself.* (Phil. 2:5–8)

These words of Paul remind us that all godly action begins with a 'renewing of the mind'. Right thinking produces right actions. Our actions are the fruit of our deepest thought; thinking and acting like Christ are a fundamental requirement for all of us.

Think of a Yoke . . . Think of a Cross . . .

These are instruments that will take away your independence and they may also take you where, humanly speaking, you would not normally choose to go.[61] Are you prepared for this?

When, like the apostle Paul, we consciously choose the way of service and genuinely seek the glory of God and the good of others, a deep change occurs within us; we become directed from a new centre and by a different source.

> *I sought my God and my God I couldn't find;*
> *I sought my soul and my soul eluded me;*
> *I sought to serve my brother in his need, and I found all three;*
> *My God, my soul and thee.*[62]

Reflection

Pause and think about this:

- To what extent does self-interest rule in your life?
- How much of your life is given to meeting the needs of others?
- How could you increase the level of your service?

CHAPTER SIX
Live By Design Not By Default
The Best Way to Set Goals

Anything less than conscious commitment to the important is an unconscious commitment to the unimportant. (Stephen Covey)[63]

Faith is the substance of things hoped for, the evidence of things not seen. (Heb. 11:1)

The pages of history recount the deeds of people whose lives were directed by a strong sense of purpose. Most of the major achievements on record are attributable to men and women with powerful dreams.

Moses, the man of God, foresaw a land of promise flowing with plenty, towards which he was leading God's people. This vision became the focus of his actions. Nehemiah, a Jewish exile who rose to occupy an important place in the administration of a foreign king, had vision. He pictured the ancient city of Jerusalem with its ruined walls rebuilt and the life of its community restored. This inspired him to act and to compel others to act with him.

Dr Martin Luther King Jr, leader of the black peoples of America, active in the struggle for justice and equality, had a vision. He voiced it on numerous occasions, the most memorable of which was during a speech he gave in Memphis, Tennessee, on 3rd April 1968, the day before his assassination:

I just want to do God's will. And He's allowed me to go up to the mountain. And I've looked over and I've seen the promised land. I may not get there with you. But I want you to know tonight that we as a people will get to the promised land. And I'm happy tonight. I'm not worried about anything. I'm not fearing any man. Mine eyes have seen the glory of the coming of the Lord.[64]

When things like vision, purpose and ideals crumble or are cast aside, we end up going through the motions and eventually become tired and are left with no purpose other than to preserve our own existence. Vision energises us. It inspires our goals and influences how we lead our lives. 'Where there is no vision, the people perish' (Prov. 29:18 KJV).

Each of us needs goals. Without them we die; in some instances literally. The internationally renowned psychiatrist Victor Frankl endured years of unspeakable horror in Nazi death camps. The incredible attempts to dehumanise man at the concentration camps of Auschwitz and Dachau led him to develop a revolutionary approach to psychotherapy known as 'logotherapy' in which the focus is on the future not the past. The method is introspective rather than retrospective and aims to get people to think about the meanings to be found and fulfilled in their lives. Referring to his experiences in the camps he says:

The prisoner who had lost his faith in the future – his future – was doomed. With his loss of belief in the future, he also lost his spiritual hold; he let himself decline and became subject to mental and physical decay. Those who know how close the connection is between the state of mind of a man – his courage and hope – or lack of them and the state of immunity of his body will understand that the sudden loss of hope and courage can have a deadly effect. The death rate in the week before Christmas, 1944 and New Year's, 1945 increased in camp beyond all previous experience. In the opinion of the chief doctor of the camp the explanation for this did not lie in the harder working conditions or the deterioration of our food supplies or a change of weather or new epidemics. It was simply that the majority of prisoners had lived in the naïve hope that they would be home by Christmas. As the time drew near and there was no encouraging news, the prisoners lost courage and disappointment overcame them. This had a dangerous effect upon their powers of resistance and a great many of them died.[65]

Human beings need goals, things to strive for and work towards. If you do not give yourself a new goal you'll most likely duplicate the one you already have and today will look a lot like yesterday! Your system needs a goal.

Having reached this point in the book, you should by now be starting to think about your own goals. Ask yourself, 'What do I want?' What do you want for yourself, for your family, your church, your community? Because of the way we have been made to function, we tend to move towards and become like what we think about. In some senses your life is a mirror reflecting your inner world. What you hold in mind comes to life irrespective of your preferences. So, why not give yourself goals that will bring you to where you want to be and live by design instead of by default?

'Live By Design Not By Default' is the title of this chapter and it is good advice. But who is the designer? Where should the Christian's life goals come from and what should they look like?

The Human Potential Movement

The story of the building of the tower of Babel, told in the Old Testament book of Genesis, describes in some ways the emergence of what we know today as the human potential movement:

> *Now the whole earth had one language and one speech. And it came to pass, as they journeyed from the east, that they found a plain in the land of Shinar, and they dwelt there. Then they said to one another, 'Come, let us make bricks and bake them thoroughly.' They had brick for stone and asphalt for mortar. And they said, 'Come, let us build ourselves a city and a tower whose top is in the heavens; let us make a name for ourselves, lest we be scattered abroad over the face of the whole earth.' But the LORD came down to see the city and the tower which the sons of men had built. And the LORD said, 'Indeed the people are one and they all have one language, and this is what they begin to do; now nothing that they propose to do will be withheld from them.'* (Gen. 11:1–6)

Human beings have huge potential whether acting together or individually and it's easy to conclude that this transcendent capacity to think, discover, discern, imagine, create and accomplish makes us invincible; that man is indeed the master of things. But this is not so. The Creator controls the creature and the concluding words of this episode are:

'Come let Us go down and there confuse their language, that they may not understand one another's speech.' So the LORD *scattered them abroad from there over the face of all the earth, and they ceased building the city.'* (Gen. 11:7–8)

From this we might learn several things that will help us to goal set and envision appropriately. First the people wanted to take the great gifts of intellect and creative power and imaginative ability that had been entrusted to them and use them for their own ends. They wanted to be famous and make a name for themselves. They feared anything that might dissipate their collective power of accomplishment and deny them the greatness they envisioned for themselves, and that same spirit has prevailed among men to this day.

The tower builders also had a number of things going for them: a common goal – they all wanted the same thing; clearly understood objectives – they all knew what the plan was; a good communication system – they all spoke the same language; shared values – they all wanted fame and notoriety; total ownership of the process – they were all committed to seeing the goal achieved, the vision realised.

This can teach us at least three things about the goals we set:

First, we must be clear about what they are. You can't hit a target you can't see. It is of fundamental importance to be as clear and precise as you possibly can about what you are setting out to accomplish. More about this later in the chapter.

Second, there is a need to be focused upon the attainment of your goals; they should fill your vision, distractions can be deadly.

Third, you need to be committed to attaining them, and this commitment has to be total and unremitting.

There is one more thing about the vision and goals we have: they must be correct. This we also learn from the tower builders of Babel. Success is not measured in terms of the goals we achieve but in the attainment of a worthy goal or the pursuit of a worthwhile vision.

'Set a goal that commands your thoughts, liberates your energy and inspires your hopes.'[66] So said Andrew Carnegie, the Scottish-American industrialist, business magnate and philanthropist, and his words, coming as they do from one of the most successful men of the post-modern world, have a certain ring of authority about them. But there's a better and a surer way to give yourself goals of the right kind; it opens up when, like the apostle Paul, you ask God to set the goal for you (Acts 9:6). We can know this as we meditate upon the Word and give ourselves to focused, meaningful prayer. As our connectedness with the ways and purposes of God develops and we continue to cultivate a servant attitude, then what we are to do and be will become clear.

When what God wants for you becomes what *you* want for you and these two things become one, that is when you will find yourself treading 'the path of life' (Ps. 16:11).

Vision and goals come in all shapes and sizes both long- and short-term but they have one thing in common: they answer the question 'What do we want?' Instead of simply reacting to events and circumstances as they arise, we need to be proactive. God Himself is working 'all things according to the counsel of His will' (Eph. 1:11), and as we work towards our own unique and specific goals we shall be working with Him, in keeping with His eternal purposes and will.

Where Do You Start?

Begin by identifying specific areas in your life where you need to set goals. By now you should have some ideas about aspects of your life where you know you need to see some change. Perhaps there are improvements you want to make, or new skills you wish to acquire. Maybe there is something you want to accomplish or you have habits and attitudes that are getting in the way that need to alter. Or is there a comfort-zone challenge you are facing?

Start by making a list! Don't just concentrate on one or two areas. Your life has many sides to it and you need to look at what is happening in each area of it. Try to get some kind of balance between them. The apostle Peter counsels believers to 'add to your faith' (2 Pet. 1:5–8) and highlights several key areas of life they should address.

Start with yourself but don't stop there. Think of others, church, family, community. Try to avoid simply creating a shopping list. A good practice is to wait patiently before God, in meditation and prayer, with your list, and the God who planted a dream in the heart of Joseph will do the same thing for you.

Your goals and the prospect of reaching them should fill you with excitement and enthusiasm. If they don't, then question seriously whether they are meant for you. These words were found inscribed on the wall of a church in Sussex, England. They date back as far as 1730:

A vision without a task is but a dream.
A task without a vision is drudgery.
A vision and a task are the hope of the world.

Goal setting is a powerful process and determines the direction in which your life will travel. Your goals will either take you back into the past, keep you where you are or they will take you forward. There is no future in going back or in staying as you are. The Bible doesn't talk about 'the good old days'! If we constantly think and talk about the past we will create for ourselves a comfort zone based on the past. 'Remember Lot's wife' (Luke 17:32).

If we only talk about the present we will be stuck where we are now and things will stay exactly the same. Nothing will change; there will be no forward movement.

If you don't set a new goal your depth mind releases just enough energy to keep things as they are. No new goals means no new energy, no new ideas, no progress. In this state you probably won't see opportunities in front of you, even though they may be staring you in the face, because your awareness has shut down. 'Lift up your eyes,' said Christ to His disciples, 'and look at the fields, for they are already white for harvest' (John 4:35).

Think about this carefully. Think about it in relation to yourself, your family, your church. Trying to maintain the status quo is never a good policy because in life nothing ever stands still. We are either going forward or going back; getting better or getting worse; improving or deteriorating.

If we think of our goals for the future as happening now we will move towards the new way, the new place, the new person God wants us to be.

> *One thing I do, forgetting those things which are behind and reaching forward to those things which are ahead, I press towards the goal for the prize of the upward call of God in Christ Jesus.* (Phil. 3:13–14)

The future beckons, it always does; set the kind of goals that move you towards it.

Goal Setting for the Future – The Rules

Rule One: Don't dwell on the problem but on the solution. The discipline must be to think about what you want in your life and not about what you don't want. Let your goal describe the outcome you want. Don't let it be a description of what you don't want.

Rule Two: Put it into words; use action words (verbs), the kind that help you picture vividly how things will look and how you will feel when the goal is reached. Also, use words that convey emotion and feelings, such as 'joyfully', 'thankfully', 'fervently'.

These are biblical words certainly, they occur frequently in the text of Scripture and convey the enthusiasm and passion that people feel in relation to attaining a specific goal, for example deliverance from a situation, worship with others, and so on. But they provide good examples of how to make a goal emotional as well as vivid, using words.

Next, use words that are precise and specific; words that pinpoint the detail and describe exactly what is envisaged by the goal. Using words this way, you give yourself a clear, precise picture, with emotion, of the goal you intend to reach.

One thing that all goals have in common is an end, something that lets us know that we have achieved them. For every goal we have we may hold a picture of it in our minds. The clarity and vividness and desirability of that picture is what determines how strong the goal is. This leads to another important matter that relates to goal setting.

Rule Three: When setting a goal you should focus only upon what the outcome is to be and not try to work out how it is to be achieved. In simple terms you set the goal before you know how to accomplish it!

Your Goal Should be Just Out of Reach But Not Out of Sight

This is a principle you should allow yourself to be guided by: when a goal is 'just out of reach' it means you know what the goal is but you don't know how to achieve it. This second part is also important: the goal must not be out of sight; you have to be able to see yourself doing, being or having what the goal describes.

At the time of the Annunciation of Christ (Luke 1:31–35), Mary's response to what the angel Gabriel proposed was, 'How can this be?' She understood clearly and vividly what the outcome of the goal was to be and her part in it, but could not see how it was to be accomplished. The angel's response is classic, 'The Holy Spirit shall come upon you and the power of the Highest will overshadow you.' This sets out a clear principle of Scripture: that which seems impossible to us is possible with God. Mary's response is also classic as she replies, 'Let it be to me according to your word' (v.38). We accept the goal. We make it our own and we go forward with a clear understanding of what it is without knowing how it will be achieved but believing that it will.

Faith is the substance of things hoped for, the evidence of things not seen. (Heb. 11:1)

So when setting a goal it is not necessary to describe or even know how it will be achieved. Once you set a new goal, that is when God has declared a new significance in your life, causing you to begin to aspire to something new, and you buy into this, that is you believe it, then your awareness opens up and you will begin to see ways of achieving it which you were not able to see before. The Holy Spirit will bring you the creativity and the energy you need to see it through to a satisfactory conclusion. The seemingly impossible task of crafting all the items needed for the Old Testament Tabernacle in the wilderness, according to the pattern God Himself had decreed, was taken on by an artisan named Bezalel. He and his fellow workers were gifted and energised by God's Spirit in a unique way that enabled them to accomplish this goal (Exod. 31:1–6).

You Get Guidance as You Get Going

The words of W.H. Murray, who led the Scottish expedition to the Himalayas in 1951, are instructive.

> *Until one is committed there is hesitancy, the chance to draw back, always ineffectiveness. Concerning all acts of initiative or creation, there is one elementary truth . . . that the moment one definitely commits oneself, then Providence moves too. All sorts of things occur to help one that would otherwise never have occurred. A whole stream of events issues from the decision, raising in one's favour all manner of incidents and meetings and material assistance which no man would have believed would have come his way. I have learned a deep respect for one of Goethe's couplets: 'Whatever you can do or dream you can do, begin it. Boldness has genius, power and magic in it.'*[67]

Rule Four: When you are setting a goal it's also vital to use words that describe it as though it had already been achieved. You speak about it and think about it as a present reality. This is using the language of faith. You speak and think of the future as though it was already here and not something you are hoping for or would like to happen. The depth mind accepts without question whatever we tell it. We must ensure that the words and the emotions that go with them reflect a passionate belief that what we are describing is fact. Not something that will yet be but something that is now. This is the way to cooperate with the Divine purpose, when you take what has been declared and turn it into a goal for you.

The famous Disney theme park ride Pirates of the Caribbean was Walt Disney's 'magnum opus'. Disney himself passed away in 1966, just one year before its grand opening. Whenever people would ask his daughters, 'Don't you wish your dad could have seen this?' they were known to have replied, 'He did!'[68]

Rule Five: Make the new goal more dominant and appealing and desirable than the old way that you are now in. Don't get preoccupied with how the goal is going to be reached or the vision fulfilled but remember that what you want must be more desirable and dominant than what you already have or where you already are.

Being able to define your goals in ways that make them clear and desirable is key because now you have two 'realities' in your mind. One describes the old scenario or present situation you are immersed in and the other is the new scenario which is defined by the new goal. The scenario that is most dominant and most desirable is the one that you will move towards.

The apostle Paul strikes a sad little note in his second letter to Timothy saying, 'Demas has forsaken me, having loved this present world' (2 Tim. 4:10). Demas clearly found the old way of the world more desirable than the new way of Christ and found a way of going back to it. Rather like Lot's wife!

How to Realise Your Goals

Form an attachment to your goal that is personal. The cliché is rather old and tired but there is some truth in it: 'if it's to be it's up to me'. Make your goal personal. If you allow yourself to think that the goal belongs to someone else or that you have no part to play in reaching it, you will tend to give up accountability and that means your awareness will shut down; you won't see opportunities that could help and you won't care. Your creativity and innovative impulses will diminish.

When you possess a new vision or goal you will begin to experience what is sometimes called the 'Divine discontent'. This is a disturbance within you; a feeling of being unsettled. You find that you just don't feel right about things the way they are.

William Booth felt this as an apprentice in a pawnbroker's shop in the city of Nottingham, England. He saw the best and worst of humanity coming through the door of the shop each day. He saw that beyond this lay a deeper and greater need that was spiritual as well as social. In his mind he cried, 'Something must be done.' In 1865 he accepted an invitation to run East London missions as a temporary ministry. After seeing some of the gin palaces he told his wife, 'I seemed to hear a voice sounding in my ears saying, "Where can you go and find such heathen as these, and where is there so great a need for your labours?"'[69] He was being stirred by the Divine discontent and the outcome of his vision and goals was the birth of what we know today as the Salvation Army.

George Muller of Bristol, England, felt stirred by the same Spirit. He saw the many thousands of orphans roaming the streets of Bristol, uncared for, undernourished, abused, uneducated and with little hope for the future. Many of his fellow Christians at that time were losing faith in God and a vision of a better way slowly developed within him. He established goals in his mind and the reality of what he envisaged and believed for materialised into what we have today. He cared for over two thousand orphaned children each year for almost fifty years and his goal, expressed in his own words, was realised:

My great desire was that it might be seen that God is still the living God and that now, as well as thousands of years ago, He listens to the prayers of His children and helps those who trust in Him.[70]

The Old Testament Patriarch Abraham 'was called to go out to the place which he would receive as an inheritance. And he went out, not knowing where he was going' (Heb. 11:8). At the age of eighty he left his home, his family and friends, his business and his associates. He left the old for the new and the rest is history.
If you want to accomplish things you've never accomplished before, you have to start doing things you've never done before.
This is the challenge that faces anyone who would live by design rather than by default and it also involves great risk. Opportunity is always accompanied by an element of risk and these two things are mutually exclusive. The place of maximum security is also the place of minimum opportunity and is commonly called the gaol. The place of maximum opportunity is also the place of minimum security and is ordinarily known as the jungle.

Most of us choose to live somewhere between the gaol and the jungle. It is for you to decide where you will settle.

Reflection

Take a few moments to explore those areas of life that are important to you today.

Personal, Family, Relationships, Social, Health, Ministry, Other

- In which of these areas do you feel God may be speaking to you and calling you to make some changes?
- Choose one and draft a simple goal or vision statement: write it as though you already were that kind of person or had that kind of relationship or ministry.
- Ask yourself, 'How much am I growing?'
- When setting goals for yourself are you guided by the same controlling desire of the apostle Paul (read 2 Cor. 5:9).

CHAPTER SEVEN
Stay Alive All Your Life!
Keeping on Track, On Fire and On Purpose

The glory of God is man, fully alive. (St Irenaeus of Lyon)[71]

You ran well. Who hindered you from obeying the truth? This persuasion does not come from Him who calls you. (Gal. 5: 7–8)

Now that you have come this far, where should you go from here? Life is a journey and our life in the Spirit is an ongoing, continuously developing experience. The observation made by humorist and social commentator Will Rogers back in the 1930s, has a serious if funny side to it. He said, 'Even if you're on the right track, you'll get run over if you just sit there!'[72]

Some Things are Part of Our History But Not Part of Our Destiny

The Old Testament Patriarch Abraham discovered that he had to leave his settled, successful place in Ur of the Chaldees in order to truly follow the One who was calling him to greater things.

In the New Testament Jesus taught a similar principle to those who wanted to follow Him. Whether to the rich young ruler enquiring about eternal life[73] or to His disciples in private conversation[74] or to the individuals who approached Him and pledged themselves to follow Him,[75] His message was the same:

173

you have to leave in order to follow; you have to let go of the old before you can take hold of the new.

The same principle applies to us. We need to learn that some things are part of our history but not part of our destiny. The words of the apostle Paul help us to see that letting go in order to move on happens when you realise this and learn to distinguish between the two.

> *Not that I have already attained or am already perfect; but I press on that I may lay hold of that for which Christ Jesus has laid hold of me . . . forgetting those things which are behind and reaching forward to those things which are ahead, I press towards the goal for the prize of the upward call of God in Christ Jesus.* (Phil. 3:12–14)

In this final chapter we'll explore the implications that these things have for us.

Staying On Track: the Sigmoid Curve

As I review my year and my life, I keep asking the same question over and over again. What am I committed to this year and for the next several years that will make me want to wake up every morning with a gusto of energy and a smile that allows me to discover my aliveness?

How do we 'stay on track'? You may have noticed in your past that sometimes as you've got closer to achieving a goal you've set, the energy and excitement you felt at the beginning of the journey seems to disappear. You just don't feel as driven to complete it and the reason is not far to seek.

I've found that for us to be energised, we need to constantly re-invent ourselves as well as our lives. We need to take on new challenges and differing roles in our life. We need to shift focus to something new or renew something old as soon as we feel our energy supplies dwindling.

I'm not proposing that we should live hedonistically, chasing every whim of sensual pleasure that we feel and abandon projects, people and hobbies when we get bored or uncomfortable. Rather, we should be aware of the plateaus that are present in our lives and notice the stage when we become stagnant and stop growing. We live out our lives in stages, and if we don't adapt to our feelings, environment and results, then we will end up moving away from our true self and what we were meant to be and do.

All things in life occur in cycles, and as nature always shows us best, most things don't grow linearly but rather cyclically – the light from the day contrasts from the darkness of night.

King Solomon, who wrote three books of the Bible, observed in one of them: 'To everything there is a season, a time for every purpose under heaven' (Ecc. 3:1).

We live our lives in seasons.

- *No season is permanent.*
- *Change, like seasons, is inevitable.*
- *Opportunities and needs, like seasons, wane as new ones begin.*

We can be purposeful, anticipating change and navigate the differing phases of our lives, or ignore it allowing circumstances to impose their changes on us.

Writer, broadcaster and teacher Charles Handy writes:

The world keeps changing. It is one of the paradoxes of life that the things and the ways which got you where you are, are seldom those that keep you there.[76]

The need to re-invent ourselves is championed by the concept of the 'Sigmoid Curve', described by Handy in his book *The Empty Raincoat*. The Sigmoid Curve is a mathematical concept that confirms the cyclical nature of everything we do in life from our relationships, careers and business lives to our personal growth.

A Sigmoid Curve looks like a stretched out 'S' lying on its side and it has 3 phases.

The Learning Phase
This is at the bottom of the S, and it rises slowly, often dipping before starting to grow. It's the initial phase of learning: the first few months of a business start-up, the first few months of a new career, or just after the honeymoon period is over in a marriage. At this stage there is a lot of hard work, no initial wins to appreciate and little sign of growth. It's here where we need the persistence and belief to push through the hard times.

The Growth Phase
There is a sharp rise in the S shape, and now things are moving quickly or we start to enjoy our relationship as it matures, and we understand each other much more. There is real growth and maturation in this phase. And we like to report our successes.

The Decline Phase

Here the line drops as the S shape begins to fall. Things start to get mundane, uninteresting and what was effortless becomes hard work. Energy levels drop as we lose the excitement of the initial stage, and we then lose focus. Things have stalled and need freshening up, and this decline can occur within a business, our careers or our Christian work and life

A good example of this is seen in the pattern that appears to repeat itself quite often in relation to the rise and decline of some political, religious and other 'movements'. First there is the *message* – the inspiration that gets things started. This is followed by the *messengers* – the men and women who believe the message, are enthused by it and who promote it fervently. Next comes the *movement* – the tangible, outward manifestation of what the message stands for and what it produces. Finally comes the *monument* – decline and stagnation set in, the energy and enthusiasm of the past seem to have departed and all that is left is an edifice, a reminder of what used to be.

Have you ever wondered why movements become monuments? The fact is that in life nothing ever stands still and the key is to negotiate its phases at the right time and avoid the decline. We need to jump off the first curve before it hits its peak and start on something new at the beginning of a new curve. However, this is no easy task. History has shown us, from the decline of the Roman Empire to the disappearance of Kodak, that the biggest risers can fall quickly and never be able to recover. But effective people are those who are ready to adapt to the ever-changing environment, always following their excitement and being strong enough to kill off what doesn't serve them anymore.

Pioneers and Settlers

The triumph of faith over flesh is described in these words:

> *Those who say such things declare plainly that they seek a homeland. And truly if they had called to mind that country from which they had come out, they would have had opportunity to return. But now they desire a better, that is, a heavenly country. Therefore God is not ashamed to be called their God, for He has prepared a city for them.* (Heb. 11:14–16)

The spirit and attitude of the pioneer differs from that of the settler. As we get closer to our goal, the gap between our present circumstances and vision we have gets smaller. The energy needed to reach it decreases and we begin to lose interest in completing it. There is a tendency to think 'this is close enough' and we settle for what we've got. But 'close enough' is never good enough. Why settle for less than what God has called you to, and has made you capable of?

The path to the future unfolds as you follow it; the vision you had at the beginning expands as you travel the road and you'll see things about your vision that you couldn't see before. You must set new goals for these. This way you 'stay on track' and avoid stagnation. But if you don't see and set the next goal on your way you come to a standstill; your goal becomes a matter of getting through the day, performing its necessary routines and progress ceases.

Staying On Fire, The Triumvirate of Hope

He will baptise you with the Holy Spirit and fire. (Luke 3:16)

How do you maintain your energy levels? How do you retain your enthusiasm for life? What is your 'fire within'? Our word 'enthusiasm' comes from two Greek words, *'en'* and *'theos'* which mean 'the God within'! Therein lies the key; the Holy Spirit is not only God with us but God within us. He is our inspiration; the source of our energy and creativity.

However, this does not put us beyond the reach of despair. Nor does it stop the clouds of despondency, even depression descending upon us at times. All of us from the least to the greatest can have times when our sense of self-worth takes a knock. Even Elijah, the great prophet and man of God, had his moments of despair: 'And he prayed that he might die, and said, "It is enough! Now, LORD, take my life, for I am no better than my fathers!"' (1 Kgs 19:4). Occasionally our own inner dialogue can sound like this.

There are several facets to your true self. They determine what you think you are worth, what you accept as good enough for you and how persistent and resilient you are in the face of the obstacles you meet.

Researchers have identified a trio of negative thoughts that occur in depression.[77] When people become depressed, they have negative views about themselves, the world and their future. They see themselves as relatively worthless, the world as a bleak place and, worst of all, they feel helpless to do anything about it. These negative thoughts often take a stereotyped and repetitive form so that the depressed person is constantly and almost 'automatically' thinking particular negative thoughts relating to the same set of circumstances which simply reinforce the scenario and, to them, confirm the 'truth' of it.

There are three beliefs that can sometimes come together in your life and when they do it can put you into a downward spiral of despondency and despair.

First: *feeling worthless.* This is your sense of self-worth, historically known as self-esteem. We must be careful not to overdo this. 'For I say . . . to everyone who is among you, not to think of himself more highly than he ought to think' *(*Rom. 12:3). By the same token we must be equally careful not to underestimate it and allow ourselves or others to put us down. We need to have a proper estimate of our own self worth. 'In lowliness of mind let each esteem others better than himself' (Phil. 2:3).

You'll discover, if you've not already found out, that we live in a society where self-worth is constantly being undermined. Here's a simple 'test' you can do. Set aside a period of time and make a promise to yourself that during this time you'll not say anything that would put another person down. If you do this you'll become aware that most of the words we use and conversations we engage in have the effect of lowering the self-worth of the other person. We see it in families, in the workplace, in churches and in communities. Sometimes it's unintentional and at other times it is deliberate. This feeling of 'worthlessness' is noticeable in prisons where low esteem is a factor in criminality. It is found in drug addicts, alcoholics and among people who have destructive lifestyles.

Second: *feeling the world is a hostile, unfriendly, fearful place where all the decisions go against you.* A loss of self-worth combined with the feeling that everything is against you can present a serious challenge to fiery enthusiasm and raise questions about the validity and worth of everything you're trying to accomplish.

Third: *feeling the future is hopeless* and that you can't do anything about it. A sense of helplessness takes hold of you.

When a combination of these thought patterns occurs within us and is sustained for a length of time we only recall times when we failed. The end result is that we expect to fail before we start. The final stage is paralysis of will. We can't find energy to do anything. We isolate ourselves and paint worst-case pictures for everything.

The fire goes out

Remember, no matter what you feel trapped by, you have power within you, through Christ, that can transform this triad of despair into a triumvirate of hope. When you use the skills that you have learned throughout this book you will start recognising these troublesome thought patterns and start controlling your inner dialogue by taking hold of the Word of God. Through correct-thinking skills based on the Word of God and inspired by His Holy Spirit, your loss of self-worth can be restored until you feel 'worth more' and you make others feel worth more too.

Meanwhile, remember you are loved by God and accepted by Him through Christ. You are unique and you have potential.

The hostile environment can become helpful, even conducive to your life and work. Remember, 'He who is in you is greater than he that is in the world' (1 John 4:4). Hopelessness can be changed to hopefulness. The fire can be rekindled and sustained.

Know Your Purpose and Stick to It

You can't stay on purpose by accident. Our challenge is to prioritise what is truly important to us. Ask yourself, 'What is my purpose?' Better still, write it out using twenty-five words or less. As we noticed earlier, this is a good discipline since if you find you can't put it into words it probably means you haven't got a purpose, or you've got a purpose but you don't understand it, or you're not yet thinking about it clearly enough. Either way, you need to know what it is.

Once you know what your purpose is ask yourself another question, 'What am I doing now?' Most of us find that there is a disconnect between what we declare is our purpose and what we find ourselves doing most of the time. We get distracted by 'other things'. Often we don't realise the full impact this has unless we pause and reflect upon what is taking place.

In 1906 an Italian economist named Vilfredo Pereto[78] created a mathematical formula to describe the unequal distribution of wealth in his country. He observed that 20 per cent of the people owned 80 per cent of the wealth. This principle that 20 per cent of something is always responsible for 80 per cent of the results became known as the Pareto principle or, more commonly, the 80/20 rule.

Here are some examples:

- Time: 20 per cent of our time produces 80 per cent of the results we want.
- Counselling: 20 per cent of the people take up 80 per cent of our time.

- Work: 20 per cent of our effort gives 80 per cent of our satisfaction.
- Leadership: 20 per cent of the people make 80 per cent of the decisions.

If you want to feel the challenge of the Pareto principle you should first make a list of the things that take up your time and use up your energy and resources. Then consider your list and think of it this way: eight out of every ten things on your list of things you do probably aren't worth doing and if you stopped doing them you wouldn't notice the difference!

The value of the Pareto principle is that it reminds you to find and focus upon the 20 per cent that matters. Of the things you do in your day only 20 per cent really matter. These 20 per cent produce 80 per cent of your results. Identify and focus on these.

Here are some lessons from the Pareto principle that will help you to 'get creative' when you're trying to stay on purpose:

Activity does not equal accomplishment
Your goal should not be simply to keep busy. Look to your purpose. Be like a postage stamp: stick to one thing until you get there! Be inspired by the philosophy of the apostle Paul who said: 'One thing I do' (Phil. 3:13).

Work smarter not harder
What good does it do to work extremely hard if it accomplishes little? Say 'no' sometimes. When you know what your gift and calling is it's a lot easier to determine the 'yes's and 'no's of life.

When a task would not further your goal you need to just say 'no'. Distractions can be dangerous! Take note of how a famous Old Testament wall builder dealt with them: 'I am doing a great work, so I cannot come down. Why should the work cease while I leave it and go down to you?' (Neh. 6:3).

Evaluate or stagnate

Determining where you stand in relation to your goals is important. Focus on where you are in relation to where you're going not where you've come from or how far you've come.

Schedule your priorities

Control your day or it will control you. Don't spend your time doing things that don't matter or that matter less. The issue is not prioritising your schedule; it is scheduling your priorities.

Stay Alive All Your Life!

There is a simple practice you can adopt that will help you 'stay on track, on fire and on purpose' throughout your lifetime.

Keep a journal.

Let's say you've got a pretty good idea of what you want in life. But you can't seem to get there. You have all these resolves: you're going to get healthy; you're going to be more present with your loved ones; you're going to be more patient and happy; you're going to be more organised; you're going to be a better friend; you're going to overcome bad habits.

But the problem is that doing these things is really hard. And it gets harder every day. Some days it seems more realistic to just give up entirely. The old 'one step forward and two steps back' pattern takes hold.

When there's a gap between who you are and who you intend to be, you are incongruent and unhappy. You're torn, mentally exhausted and regretful. You always feel slightly like a fraud to yourself, and probably to the people around you.

If you try to tackle everything wrong in your life, you'll quickly burn-out and quit. It's happened many times before. Life is busy; you just don't have time to focus on a thousand different areas of your life to change. That's exhausting and, frankly, not helpful.

The Need for a Powerfully Transformative Keystone Habit

More effective than microscopically analysing your sabotaging behaviours is for you to develop a 'keystone' habit, which tightly locks all your other habits in place. Without the keystone, everything falls apart.

In his book *The Power of Habit*, Charles Duhigg describes keystone habits as 'small changes or habits that people introduce into their routines that unintentionally carry over into other aspects of their lives'.[79]

Keystone habits spark a chain reaction of other good habits and can rapidly alter every aspect of your life, and keeping a daily journal is one of the most potent keystone habits you can acquire. If you do it properly, you will show up better in every area of your life. Here are some examples:

Keeping a journal creates a springboard for daily recovery

We struggle to detach ourselves from work. More now than ever, we fail to live in the present moment. Our family and friends are lucky to catch a small percentage of our attention while they're with us.

Journal sessions are a time to reflect. Note what you got done that day and what needs to be moved to tomorrow. Write the things you learned and experienced. Direct your subconscious by writing about things you want to focus on tomorrow. As you put work behind you for the evening, your subconscious will go to work and prepare you for tomorrow.

Keeping a journal generates clarity and consistency

By writing in your journal you'll quickly see the inconsistencies in your life such as what needs to be removed and what should be included in your life. Journaling is a powerful facilitator of self-discovery. Not only will you have more clarity about your path in life, but journaling improves your ability to make small and large decisions along the way.

Keeping a journal clears your emotions

When you are in an intensely emotional mood, when you write about how you feel it can help you more fully experience and understand those emotions.

Keeping a journal helps you to learn

We're bad at retaining information. We forget most of what we read and hear. However, when you write down the things you've learned, you retain them far better. Even if you never re-read what you've written, the simple act of writing something down increases brain development and memory.

Neurologically, when you listen to something a different part of your brain is engaged than when you write it down. Memory recorded by listening does not discriminate important from non-important information. But writing creates spatial regions between important and non-important pieces of information allowing your memory to target and ingrain the important stuff you want to remember. Furthermore, the act of putting things into words allows your subconscious mind to work out problems in unique ways, intensifying the learning process and giving you insights while you ponder and write about the things you're learning.

Keeping a journal increases your gratitude!
Even if you start a journal session in a bad mood, the insight writing brings has a subtle way of shifting your mind towards gratitude.

When you start writing what you're grateful for, new chambers of thought open in your mind. You'll often need to put your pen down and take a few overwhelming breaths. You'll be captivated not only by the amazing things in your life, but by the awe and brilliance of life in general. Make sure you include things to be grateful for when you write in your journal each day.

Strategies to Enhance the Experience of Keeping a Journal

- Pray or meditate for inspiration before you begin, to heighten your mental state and trigger creativity.

- Write about the people in your life; you'll get breakthroughs about how to improve those relationships.
- Write with confidence and power; use this to strengthen your resolve.
- Write *'This is the day the LORD has made; we will rejoice and be glad in it'* (Ps.118:24). If that doesn't inspire you, find another translation of it that does and read it over and over until you begin to believe it!
- If you can't think of what to write, try writing about minute details of your day or recent history.

A journal begins as an empty book but writing in a journal can make your life come alive. It's a practice that fosters intimate, personal learning. Set aside some time each day to write down what you think about yourself. Reflect quietly on the way you feel things are going with your life, your work, your relationships, your ministry, and so forth.

Use the reflective section at the close of each chapter of this book and, in particular, the content of this final chapter, to stir your thought processes and help you think about where you are now with different aspects of your life, and also where you are going. You'll become aware of the parts of your life that are incomplete.

Sir Francis Bacon observed that 'writing maketh an exact man'. By writing these reflections down you give yourself a sound, accurate base from which you'll be able to make better decisions about who you are and what you want.

Take these thoughts with you when you meditate and pray, when you seek guidance and when you ponder over the direction of your life and your ministry of service as discussed in chapter five. Let these all important spiritual disciplines be the means of discovering your condition and pointing the way forward for you.

The word of God is living and powerful, and sharper than any two-edged sword, piercing even to the division of soul and spirit; and is a discerner of the thoughts and intents of the heart. (Heb 4:12–13)

In the final analysis, let your journal be something that reflects what God Himself is saying to you and requiring of you and even of how He wants to lead you.

Keep Hope Alive

Ours is a journey that takes us 'through all the changing scenes of life, in sorrow and in joy'.[80] It is a fluid, dynamic experience in which nothing stands still.

You do not know what will happen tomorrow. For what is your life? It is even a vapour that appears for a little time then vanishes away. Instead you ought to say, 'If the Lord wills, we shall do this or that.' (Jas. 4:14–15)

Life is short and uncertain, but despite this it is also full of possibilities both good and bad.

To each is given a bag of tools
A shapeless mass, a book of rules;
And each must make ere time has flown –
A stumbling block or a stepping stone.[81]

How will you be remembered? What kind of legacy will you leave?

This book has addressed the question of effective living from a Christian perspective and given Christian answers.

The question is often asked, 'Do these ideas work?' The short answer is 'No!' No idea works of itself; but we do! We can only ask of an idea or principle the question, 'Is it true?' The ideas and concepts of this book are true not just because they are psychologically sound, and this can be proved but, more importantly, because they are biblically based.

The question you must ask of yourself is 'Am I willing to apply them?' Only you can answer this. My task, through this book, is to see that you know how. The rest is up to you.

Live by design, not by default, and may you find joy in your journey.

Endnotes

Preface

1.Govan gets it right: The Sunday Herald 26 Oct. 1995

2. Readers Digest. Vol. 87. 1965

Introduction

3. 'By Cool Siloam's Shady Rill' written by Reginald Heber (1783–1826). Public Domain.

4. Jessie B. Rittenhouse, 'My Wage', *The Door of Dreams* (1918), p.25.

Chapter One

5. William Barclay, *The Mind of Jesus* (SCM Press Ltd, 2012), p.9.

6. William Shakespeare, *Macbeth*, act 5, scene 5.

7. John Stott, *Your Mind Matters: The Quest for Holiness* (Inter-Varsity Press, 2007), p.33–34.

8. Romans 6:3,16; 1 Corinthians 3:16; 5:6; 6:2,3,9,15,16,19.

9. John Stott, *Your Mind Matters*, p.33–34.

10. Cited in Dale Carnegie, *How to Stop Worrying and Start Living* (Cedar, 1993, copyright © 1984 Donna Dale Carnegie and Dorothy Carnegie) chapter 19.

11. Acts 9:15; 2 Corinthians 4:7.

12. Eugene H. Peterson, 'Growth: An Act of the Will?' *Christianity Today* (Fall, 1988), www.christianitytoday.com.

13. Rick Warren, *The Purpose Driven Life: What on Earth Am I Here For?* (Zondervan, 2013). Day 1: 'It All Begins with God'.

14. J.M. Barrie (1860–1937), *The Little Minister*, chapter1: 'The Love-light'.

15. Dr Martin Luther King Jr, *Strength to Love* (Fortress Press, 2010), chapter 2, 'Transformed Nonconformist'.

16. Romans 12:2 PHILLIPS.

17. Stephen R. Covey, *The Seven Habits of Highly Effective People: The Power*

of a Paradigm Shift (Simon and Schuster, 2004).

18. William Carey (1761–1834), quoted in *The Baptist Herald and Friend of Africa*, October 1842 and in 'The Missionary Herald', *The Baptist Magazine* vol. 35, January 1843.

19. William James (1842–1910), *The Principles of Psychology Volume 1* (originally published in 1910), chapter 10: 'The Consciousness of Self'.

20. Dr Martin Luther King Jr, 'Rediscovering Lost Values', sermon delivered at Detroit Baptist Church, 28 February 1954.

Chapter Two

21. Paice L., 'Overspill Policy and the Glasgow Slum Clearance Project in the Twentieth Century', *Reinvention: a Journal of Undergraduate Research* vol. 1, issue 1(2008).

22. Eugene Peterson, *Eat This Book: A Conversation in the Art of Spiritual Reading* (Hodder & Stoughton, 2008).

23. Eugene Peterson, https://quotefancy.com.quote.eugenepeterson

Chapter Three

24. Leo Tolstoy, 'Three methods of Reform' in *Pamphlets: Translated from the Russian* (1900).

25. Exodus 28:3; 1 Chronicles 28:12.

26. Ezekiel 11:5; 20:32.

27. Cf. 1 Chronicles 22:19; 28:9.

28. Romans 1:28; Ephesians 4:17–18.

29. Romans 8:7; Colossians 1:21

30. James Allen, *As a Man Thinketh*, reprint edition (first published in 1902), (TarcherPerigee, 2006).

31. 'My Robot: R-U-ME2', in Denis Waitley, *The Psychology of Winning* (Warner Books, 1992).

Chapter Four

32. Stephen R. Covey, *Principle-centred Leadership* reissue edition (Simon &

Schuster, 1999), chapter 8: 'Moral Compassing'.

33. Dr Martyn Lloyd-Jones, *Spiritual Depression: Its Causes and Cures* (Zondervan, 1998), p.20–21.

34. Genesis 3:3.

35. Luke 4:4,8,10.

36. Cited by Garth Lean in *Frank Buchman: A Life* (Constable, 1985), chapter 44, 'Finding Time to Die', p.529.

37. Norman Vincent Peale, *The Positive Way to Change Your Life* (Cedar Books, 2012), chapter 16: 'The Most Important Image of All'.

38. Betty Lee Skinner, *Daws: A Man Who Trusted God* (NavPress, 1993).

Chapter Five

39. Joshua 1:8; Psalm 1:2–3.

40. James 5:16.

41. Psalm 73:24.

42. Philippians 2:7; Matthew 20:26.

43. C.S. Lewis, *Letters to Malcolm: Chiefly on Prayer* (London: Geoffrey Bles, 1964), p.109. Copyright © 1964, 1963 by C.S. Lewis Pte. Ltd. Copyright renewed 1992, 1991 by Arthur Owen Barfield.

44. C.S. Lewis, *Mere Christianity* (HarperCollins, 1997) p.163. Copyright © C.S. Lewis Pte Ltd, 1942, 1943, 1944.

45. Andrew Murray, *With Christ in the School of Prayer* (Greenville SC: Ambassador Publications 1998) p.215.

46. Dietrich Bonhoeffer, *The Cost of Discipleship*, new edition (SCM Press, 2015). Copyright © 1959 by SCM Press Ltd.

47. Alfred, Lord Tennyson (1809–1892), 'Morte D'Arthur', *Idylls of the King*.

48. See also Matthew 21:21–22.

49. Genesis 37:23–28; 39:17–20; 40:23.

50. Genesis 41:41–45; 45:4–7.

51. Genesis 37:5–11.

52. Genesis 45:4–7.

53. Genesis 49:22–24.

54. Genesis 39:2–5; 21–23; 2 Samuel 6:11–12.

55. Psalm 119:105; 2 Timothy 3:15.

56. Acts 8:29; Romans 8:14.

57. Acts 11:28–29; Acts 21:4.

58. Esther 4:14; 1 Corinthians 16:8–9.

59. Proverbs 12:15; Galatians 1:16.

60. Colossians 3:15; Acts 20:22–23.

61. Matthew 11:29; John 21:18–19

62. William Blake (1757–1827).

Chapter Six

63. Stephen R. Covey, A. Roger Merrill and Rebecca R. Merrill, *First things First* (Simon & Schuster, 1994), chapter 2: 'The Addiction Urgency'.

64. Dr Martin Luther King Jr, speech given on 3rd April 1968, cited in Coretta Scott King, *The Words of Martin Luther King, Jr* (Newmarket Press, 2005).

65. Victor Frankl, *Man's Search for Meaning* (Rider, 2004), part one: 'Experiences in a Concentration Camp', p.95–97. Copyright © Victor E. Frankl 1959, 1962, 1984, 1992, 2004.

66. Andrew Carnegie (1835-1919): cited from, www.azquotes.com

67. W.H. Murray, *The Scottish Himalayan Expedition 1951* (Dent, 1951). The Goethe couplet referred to is a loose translation of Goethe's *Faust*, lines 214–30.

68. Cited from Brian Krosnick, 'From Ride to Screen', www.themeparktourist.com (15th April 2018).

69. William Booth (1829–1912), 'Christian History' in *Christianity Today*, issue 26 (1990). https://www.christianitytoday.com/history/people/activists/william-booth.html

70. G. Fred Bergin, *Ten Years After: A Sequel to the Autobiography of George Muller* (Nisbet, 1911), Introduction, p.11.

Chapter Seven

71. St Irenaeus of Lyon, *Against Heresies* (AD 185), book 4, chapter 34, section 7.

72. R. Scott Frothingham, *The Words and Wisdom of Will Rogers* (2013).

73. Luke 18:18–22.

74. Luke 9:23–24.

75. Luke 9:57–62.

76. Charles Handy, *The Empty Raincoat* (Random House, 1995), chapter 3: 'The Sigmoid Curve'.

77. Aaron Beck et al, *Cognitive Therapy of Depression* (New York: Guilford Press, 1979).

78. Vilfredo Pareto: https.//en.m.wikipedia.org/wiki/Vilfredo_Pareto

79. Charles Duhigg: *The Power of Habit* (Random House, 2012), Part Two: 'The Habits of Successful Organisations', chapter 4: 'Keystone Habits'.

80. 'Through All the Changing Scenes of Life' written by Nahum Tate (1652–1715) and Nicholas Brady (1639–1726). Public Domain.

81. Robert Lee Sharpe (1872–1951), 'A Bag of Tools'.